Bilbao

Footprint

Andy Symington

& the Basque country

Contents

Listings

About the author

Andy hails from Australia and lives in Northern Spain. In his prowls around the world he has been involved in community theatre, archaeology and selling whisky to the Scots, among other dubious activities. He now works as a freelance writer and is the author of several guidebooks, including *Footprint Northern Spain* and *Footprint Andalucía*.

Acknowledgements

As well as all the people who helped put the first edition together, for this second edition I owe particular thanks to Edgar Reina, a man with an encyclopaedic knowledge of the Bilbao eating and drinking scene, and Amalia Garrido, a back-streets guide to Vitoria. I also thank Ian Johnston, who drove a long way for a few Bilbao *zuritos*, the excellent Footprint editorial team, and my parents for their support. And Begoña García de León, for sharing the *pintxos*.

For a city that was, until relatively recently, known mostly for steel, smog and stevedores, Bilbao's transformation to cultural capital has been remarkable. Or rather, would have been remarkable, if it hadn't been achieved by the Basques, who, for several millennia, have excelled in high achievement against the odds. Number one on any list of Bilbao highlights is the city's vibrant inhabitants.

The Guggenheim Museum is an obvious symbol of the city's rejuvenation and is, indeed, spectacular: a sinuous fantasy of a building that can literally take the breath away. It inspires not only in itself but also because of the vision it took to put it there. This vision is nothing new, however; Bilbao is the main city in one of the EU's most prosperous regions; a port that, from its inception, looked outward to northern Europe and the north Atlantic rather than inward towards Madrid. Bustling bar-life, harmonious architecture, a superb eating culture and a tangible working city's pride were all here long before the Guggenheim was even imagined.

Emerging from the shadows

For 40 years under Franco, Basqueness was suppressed: the language was banned and the history was falsified. Since the end of the dictatorship, Basque culture has bounced back. The indigenous language, Euskara (Euskera) is spoken increasingly widely and, wherever you look, there are concerts, poetry readings, political rallies and other inspiring events for which much of the rest of western Europe seems to have lost the energy. This spirit affects day-to-day life here: even the semi-resident drizzle fails to dampen the Bilbaínos' mood overmuch; all the more reason to seek refuge in a café or bar and discuss the state of the world or the local football team.

Basque separateness

Despite the Basque authorities' best efforts, terrorism still grabs more column inches in the foreign press than any other issue. It's a serious business but shouldn't cloud visitors' judgement. ETA, the separatist group which has been responsible for much violence in its 50-odd years of existence (see p235), has been severely weakened in the early years of the 21st century and harming tourists in the Basque region is emphatically not on its agenda; nearly all of ETA's actions have been targeted either at the Madrid government or at any Basques who are seen as collaborators. The vast majority of Basques deplore terrorism but this doesn't mean that they don't feel strongly about independence: many do, and they shouldn't be confused with *etarristas*. Basque nationalism is a completely different issue to Basque terrorism.

'Basque'-ing in reflected glory

If Bilbao has struggled to re-invent itself, San Sebastián appears to have coasted along on the back of its superb natural setting, a magnet for beachbound visitors since the mid-19th century. Considered one of Spain's most beautiful cities, its popularity with backpackers has injected a much needed dose of youth

The name game

Castilian Spanish is the main language of the Basque lands, spoken by everyone, but, after decades hiding under Franco, the Basque language, Euskara (Euskera), has re-emerged and an ever-growing number of people are learning and using it. You'll see it everywhere, on road signs, in bars, on posters, and some of the regional towns use only Basque for naming streets. Towns in the region have both Basque and Spanish names, although there are few hard and fast rules about usage: Vitoria is usually written Vitoria/Gasteiz and San Sebastián is known as both Donostia and San Sebastián; Laguardia is hardly ever called Biazteri, while Salvatierra is often just labelled Agurain on maps. In this guide we have given both versions in headings but tended to use the Spanish only in other text. See also p237.

into the gracefully ageing resort. In contrast to both, Vitoria is a retiring beauty, a quiet achiever combining attractiveness with intelligence, and a surprising but suitable capital of the Basque lands. Away from the cities, the traditional elements which make a Basque's heart beat faster are all still part of rural life: the green hills, the colourful fishing fleets, the sloping roofs on stone farmhouses built to last, the *pelota*, the berets.

At a glance

The Basque semi-autonomous region is divided into three provinces; Bilbao/Bilbo is the capital of Vizcaya/Bizkaia province, San Sebastián/Donostia of Guipúzcoa/Guipuzkoa and Vitoria/Gasteiz of Alava/Araba. The three cities have the feeling of a council about them: distinct personalities united by their different talents and natures in order to make the combined whole stronger and wiser. All three are Basque; all three are Spanish. It's a curious duality of which Basque nationalists are wary, but which is an important factor in the liberal and exciting atmosphere that the visitor can enjoy.

Bilbao

Bilbao still visibly and proudly wears a blue collar, despite the wealth that industry has brought to large parts of the community, and the city's rapid transformation from polluted urban wasteland to ambitious riverside cultural destination. In the language of sweeping travelogue generalizations, it's a city of contrasts; from the middle of Bilbao's business district you can frequently see farmhouse-studded green hills to the left and right, while, at the estuary mouth, wealthy Getxo harbours luxury yachts within a chimney's belch of some seriously heavy waterside industry.

Casco Viejo (Old Town)

Bilbao's Casco Viejo is a case in point. Its web of attractive streets still evokes a cramped medieval past but designer clothing stores occupy the ground floors where families perhaps once huddled behind the city walls. Earthy bars serve up glasses of gutsy wine and delicious *tortilla* from a generations-old family recipe while the *pintxos* on offer next door are imaginative and tasty combinations of goose liver and fresh artichoke. Although most Bilbaínos live and work elsewhere in the city, it's still here that they congregate to chat, stroll, laugh and relax.

Riverbank

This is the most obvious beneficiary of Bilbao's leap into the 21st century: Calatrava's eerily skeletal bridge and Gehry's exuberant Guggenheim museum bring art and architecture together, making the Nervión river the city's axis once more. Ongoing work aims to further soften the remaining industrial edges and the re-established tramline now cruises along beside the riverfront promenades.

El Ensanche

The new town, El Ensanche, has an elegant European feel to it. The wealth of the city is evident here, with stately banks and classy shops lining its avenues. Although you can stride across its width in a quarter of an hour, it's divided into barrios: the studenty Indautxu, the besuited Abando. At weekends, families roam the shops, and the bars and discos crank up for all-night action.

Getxo and around

Bilbao's seaside suburbs, once reached after hours of painstaking river navigation by sweating steersmen, are now a nonchalant 20 minutes away by Metro. Fashionable Getxo has a relaxed beachy atmosphere while, across the estuary, Portugalete is still wondering how Bilbao gets all the credit these days: for hundreds of years it was a far more important port.

El País Vasco/Euskadi

Basque coastline

Mundaka and Getaria are picturesque places to visit, while Bermeo, Lekeitio and Ondarroa are important fishing ports that preserve the Basques' long-standing connection with the sea. And, Gernika has poignant reminders of its martyrdom at Franco's hands.

San Sebastián/Donostia

Rather like an aristocrat who once worked in 'suitable' employment just to bide time while waiting for his inheritance, San Sebastián has left its days as a significant port far behind. Ever since royalty summered here in the 19th century, the city has settled into its role of elegant seaside resort to the manner born. With a superb natural setting, sandy beaches, stellar restaurants and a regular influx of global stars during its film festival, it's a relaxed place, recently invigorated by excellent museums and the world-class architecture of the Kursaal auditorium.

Around San Sebastián

East of the city, Pasaia and Hondarribia are appealing coastal towns on the route to France, while inland, medieval towns such as Oñati and Elorrio preserve the region's architectural heritage. The green hills and rocky peaks of rural Euskadi are an invitation to enjoy the open air.

Vitoria/Gasteiz

Vitoria is the quiet achiever of the city trio. It comes as a surprise to discover that this peaceful town is the capital of the Basque region, but the youthful population is vocally Basque and the city feels energized as a result. The attractive old town is combined with an Ensanche that provides plenty of green spaces for its inhabitants.

Alava/Araba Province

Laguardia is one of the most attractive walled towns in northern Spain and an important centre of the Rioja wine region. There's excellent walking in Alava, whose rural areas are home to a variety of wildlife. Stray off the main routes and it's easy to find an untouched tract of land to call your own.

Trip planner

How you spend your time in the Basque lands depends on your perspective. A Bilbaíno was asked his opinion and after a few minutes of deep thought, came up with the following: "If you have two days, spend a day in San Sebastián and a day in Bilbao. If you have a month, spend a day in San Sebastián and the rest in Bilbao."

The best time to visit is also determined by your priorities. The coast has a very high annual rainfall; the driest, hottest months are July and August, but it's difficult to find accommodation at this time and prices rise, especially in the resort towns. The best compromise is to go around May or October, but expect drizzle; the emerald green of the Basque countryside doesn't come for free.

You may want to time your trip around a specific festival (see p197) – Bilbao's Semana Grande in August, or the Rioja harvest in early October, for example – but be sure to reserve accommodation beforehand. Transport and business hours are often hugely affected by local and national holidays.

The Basque country is very expensive compared with much of Spain, particularly in the eating and drinking department. Accommodation is better value for couples than solo travellers but several of the smaller towns lack viable budget options. On €50 a day a single person will get a room in a cheap *pensión*, a set meal at lunchtime, some *pintxos* or tapas in the evening, a few drinks and coffees, a couple of sights plus bus or train fares around the region. For €80 per day, you'll get a night in a good *pensión* and you won't be counting pennies. With €150 per day, you'll be very comfortable indeed.

Short breaks (two to four days)

If you've only got two days, spend them in Bilbao. While it lacks the memorable natural setting of San Sebastián and Vitoria's picturesque appeal, it's vibrant and honest and the premier symbol of the region's rejuvenation and pride in post-Franco Spain. The Guggenheim Museum is a world-class sight on a par with the Golden Gate Bridge or the Sydney Opera House. Gernika and Mundaka are both within easy reach for half-day excursions; Gernika's Museo de la Paz is a particularly worthwhile destination.

With a little longer at your disposal, you might want to spend two days in Bilbao and a day in San Sebastián, with, perhaps, a stop in Lekeitio or another coastal town in between for fresh grilled fish and beach time. Or you could head down to Alava Province and spend a night in Laguardia to enjoy a bit of wine tasting.

City lovers might want to devote their time to the three provincial capitals: an easily achievable aim given the good connections. A day each in San Sebastián and Vitoria will give you a feel for their charms; Bilbao deserves two days, if you have enough time.

Longer breaks (a week or more)

With a week to spare, you could base yourself in Bilbao for the entire time and take day trips to San Sebastián and Vitoria: hit the former if you fancy beaches, sunsets over the water and style; choose the latter for peace, Basqueness and class.

If you don't mind moving about, your trip should really include Laguardia, especially if you are a fan of wine and medieval villages; it's a gem. The inland hill towns such as Oñati and Elorrio are proudly Basque, have a noble architectural inheritance and are both good spots for striking out with a pair of sturdy boots and a picnic. Basque heritage is divided between these hills, with their distinctive *baserri* farmhouses, and the coast, with its plethora of fishing villages. The beautiful harbours at historic Lekeitio, Getaria and Hondarribia are worth visiting, as is the tiny surfing mecca of Mundaka. Any of the beaches could be enjoyed either on a night's stopover or during a relaxing stay of a few days.

Contemporary Bilbao

It's official: Europe's oldest people have been reborn and everywhere the visitor looks there's some celebration or affirmation that it's good to be Basque again. Euskadi is back on the map and the old feeling that Bilbao is the centre of the world has returned.

It's difficult to exaggerate the vibrancy that animates day to day life here. The Basque language, banned during Franco's dictatorship and in danger of a lingering death, has been reclaimed by the young and is now widely spoken in the streets by an ever-increasing number of locals. There's a touching and understandable feeling that everything Basque is good: to walk into a bookshop to see Tintin and Captain Haddock foiling villains in streams of Euskara gives an idea of how things have changed in three decades.

It seems that everything has been imbued with this 'new Basque' spirit, part of which strives to make the differences between Euskadi and Spain as evident as possible. In this sense, the Guggenheim Museum was the perfect project: a daring building that would put Bilbao on the map, attract tourism, add to Basque pride and blow a raspberry at conservative Madrid. The ruling Basque nationalists gambled that the massive investment would pay off; they were right. Public architecture here has changed for good: construction of the Guggenheim was followed by the eerily beautiful Kursaal in San Sebastián and the gleaming Artium in Vitoria. Skeletal Calatrava bridges grace the region's rivers and even the wineries of baked Rioja have commissioned extraordinary lodges in which to receive visitors.

Side by side with architectural inventiveness has marched the revival in Basque art. You can't spend more than half an hour in the region without coming across the work of the two late giants of 20th-century Basque sculpture: the fluid emotion of Oteiza or Chillida's twisting explorations of space. These two very different personalities (see p91) were rightly considered as ambassadors who carried Basque culture far outside Euskadi. The appreciation of Basque artists and the promotion of young writers, painters and actors is all part of the wave: readings of new Euskara poetry are frequent and popular.

If one aspect of Basque life is guaranteed to delight first-time visitors, it's the food or, more accurately, the food culture. From about half-past seven in the evening until midnight or so, everyone lives in the street, walking, talking, drinking and eating *pintxos*. Walk into a bar in any Basque city or village and the counter will be laden with snacks, from a traditional slice of tortilla to a sleek designer creation. Basque restaurants are, and always have been, superb, and this way of snacking has an irresistible appeal.

While other traditional Basque activities such as *pelota*, stone-lifting and log-chopping are far from being anachronisms, the two things that make modern Euskadi tick are politics and football, which are often indistinguishable. Athletic Bilbao and, to a lesser extent, Real Sociedad and Alavés regularly carry the Basque flag into battle against the Spanish enemy. Athletic only employs Basque players, who approach every game like an international. During the Franco years supporting Los Leones was one of the few ways to show Basqueness and the team remains a potent symbol.

However, the revival of Basque culture is not problem-free, despite what the slogans might have you believe. A child schooled in Euskara effectively learns Spanish as a foreign language, thus potentially jeopardizing its chance of continuing to study in the nation's tertiary system or abroad. Many Basques feel that promoting nationalism in this way can all too easily create insularity; an undesirable effect especially in a period when Spain itself is becoming increasingly outward-looking and multicultural.

Politically, the three Basque provinces are semi-autonomous; their parliament has the right to generate its own taxes, among other things. Although most Basques see this constitutional arrangement as the best way to pursue either nationalist or federalist goals, the minority that supports a more radical route to freedom is significant. ETA, the terrorist group responsible for over 800 deaths in the last 40 years, is still in evidence, although substantially weakened by a (worryingly undemocratic) crackdown by the former Partido Popular government. In August 2002, after a purpose-built bill was resoundingly passed in parliament, the courts banned Batasuna, the political party frequently seen as being linked to ETA. This was followed by a wave of arrests that severely affected ETA's resolve and capability to do damage. Frequently overlooked is the large Spanish population of the Basque provinces, who are caught in a situation that is not of their making and from which they have precious little to gain. The most divisive issue is that of Basque prisoners: the Spanish government has a deliberate policy of putting them in prisons on the other side of the country, thus making it very difficult for them to have contact with family and friends. Nearly all Basques are outraged by this; you'll see posters demanding that they be relocated to prisons closer to home (*"Euskal Presoak Euskal Herrira!"* is the most common slogan; it means "Basque prisoners to the Basque Country"). See also p235.

★ Ten of the best

Best

1 **Bilbao's Casco Viejo** It's tiny but you get lost in it. It's got shops, accommodation, architecture, Basqueness and some seriously good bars, p33.

2 **Calatrava's uplifting bridges** in Bilbao and Ondarroa, p42 and p77. He can even make airports beautiful.

3 **Guggenheim Museum** Yes, it's good, even when it's closed. The merits of the art change according to what's on show but the building is an inspiration, p43.

4 **Mundaka** A beautiful little place, home of the lost wave but still a great spot, p66.

5 **Gernika** Melancholy shrine to one of Europe's bloodiest slaughters? Not a bit of it. A cheerful and vibrant Basque market town, with a brilliant museum, p69.

6 **Lekeitio, Ondarroa or Getaria** A Basque fishing town is a very characterful thing, p73, p77 and p78.

7 **Arantzazu Monastery** The Pope wasn't happy, Franco probably wasn't happy, but this visionary building managed to combine the works of some of the best 20th-century Basque artists of the time. And if you don't like it, you can always take a walk in the superb hills around it, p101.

8 **Vitoria** A fine city, growing into its role as capital of the Basque country, p103.

9 **Laguardia** If you had a perfect medieval hilltop village, where would you put it? Slap bang in the middle of top wine country, of course. What more could you want? p116.

10 **Eating in San Sebastián** Whether it be a gourmet Michelin-starred banquet, a massive feed in a cider house, or a *pintxo* crawl through the old town, p167.

The ★ symbol is used throughout the text to indicate these recommended sights and attractions.

The main international airport in Basque Spain is Sondika, Bilbao. It's a beautiful brand new building designed by Santiago Calatrava, seemingly in homage to the whale, and is located 10 km northeast of the city centre. The cheapest direct flights from the UK tend to be with the budget operators, although scheduled flights with international airlines may work out cheaper if you want to fly at the weekend with less than a month's notice.

Bilbao and the Basque region can also be reached by ferry, bus and train from the UK. These methods of transport are unlikely to save you money but they can be a pleasurable alternative if you've enough time to spare. They also have the added advantage of allowing you to stop along the way.

Public transport in the Basque region is excellent, both within and between cities, but if you plan to explore the countryside in any depth, a car will prove invaluable, particularly if time is limited. Hiring a car in Spain is inexpensive.

Getting there

Air

From the UK and the rest of Europe The cheapest flights to Bilbao (BIO) from the UK are often with **Easyjet**, which has a daily service from London Stansted (STN). Ticket prices can be as low as £30 return but are more usually £60-120; it's easier to get hold of a cheaper fare if you fly off-season or midweek and if you book well in advance. **Ryanair** has budget routes from London Stansted to Vitoria (VIT), Santander (SDR), with a connecting bus service to Bilbao, and Biarritz (BIQ) in France, from where it's 30 minutes by train to the Spanish border and another 30 minutes to San Sebastián. Bilbao is also served from the UK by **Iberia** and **British Airways**. APEX fares tend to be about £110-140 return and can be more economical than the budget airlines if you're flying from another British city. These scheduled airlines also offer greater flexibility.

Bilbao is directly connected with several other European cities on scheduled flights, including Frankfurt, Zürich, Brussels, Paris and Milan. The airlines on these routes often have reasonable prices for connections from London: try **Lufthansa** or **Air France**. There are direct budget flights from Dublin with **Aer Lingus**, while **Air Berlin** connects Bilbao with several German and Austrian destinations via their Palma de Mallorca hub. Check www.whichbudget.com for the latest information on routes.

Connecting via other Spanish cities is another option. **Iberia** links Bilbao with most major Spanish cities, while **Spanair** and **Air Europa** also operate some flights. Tickets are fairly expensive, with a typical Madrid-Bilbao return costing about €150 but last-minute specials can bring the price down to as low as €50 and, if you're flying into Madrid from outside Spain, the onward domestic flights are often added at little extra cost. There are also flights from Madrid to San Sebastián and Vitoria.

→ Airlines and flight agents

Aer Lingus T 0818-365000, www.aerlingus.com
American Airlines T 1-800 433 7300, www.aa.com
Air Berlin T 030-410 215 903, www.airberlin.com
Air France T 0845-0845 111, www.airfrance.com
British Airways T 0845-77 333 77, www.britishairways.com
Delta T 1-800 241 4141, www.delta.com
Easyjet T 0870-6 000 000, www.easyjet.com
Iberia T 0845-601 2854, www.iberia.es
Lufthansa T 0845-7737 747, www.lufthansa.com
Ryanair T 0871-246 0000, www.ryanair.com
US Airways T 1-800 622 1015, www.usairways.com

Dial-a-flight T 0870-333 4488, www.dialaflight.com
Ebookers T 0870-050 0808, www.ebookers.com
Expedia T 0870-010 7000, T 0870-050 0808, www.expedia.com, www.expedia.co.uk
Kelkoo www.kelkoo.co.uk
Opodo www.opodo.com
STA Travel T 0870-1600 599, www.statravel.com
Which budget? www.whichbudget.com

From North America There are no direct flights to Bilbao from North America, so it's best to fly to Madrid, Barcelona, London or Paris and catch an onward connection there. From the east coast flights can rise to about US$1500 in summer but in winter or with advance purchase a return to Madrid can be as low as US$400. Tickets from the west coast are usually only US$100 or so more than the east coast price. **Iberia** flies direct to Madrid from many east coast cities; other airlines offering reasonable fares are **American Airlines**, **Delta** and **US Airways**.

Airport information **Bilbao Airport** (BIO/LEBB; **T** 905-505505) is compact and easily negotiated. There are ATMs, a tourist information point, a café, restaurant and a few shops. An efficient and cheap (€1.15) bus service runs between the airport terminal and Plaza Moyúa in central Bilbao every half hour and takes 20-30 minutes. A taxi between the airport and the centre costs about €15-20. The region's other airports are **San Sebastián-Fuentarrabia Airport** (EAS/LESO; **T** 943-668500), and **Vitoria International Airport** (VIT/LEVT; **T** 945-163591).

Rail

The main rail gateway to the Basque country from the rest of Europe is Paris Austerlitz. The daily Paris-Madrid sleeper stops at Vitoria, with a standard tourist class fare costing €100-110 one way in a reclinable seat; check www.elipsos.com for specials. The cheaper option is to take a TGV from Paris to Hendaye, on the border, from where you can catch a Spanish train to San Sebastián and beyond.

Travelling from the UK by **Eurostar** (**T** 0870-160 6600 in the UK, www.eurostar.com) to Paris Gare du Nord, then changing stations and boarding a TGV to Hendaye, can have you in San Sebastián 10 to 11 hours after leaving Waterloo, if the connections are kind. Once across the Channel, trains are reasonably priced but factor in £100-200 return on Eurostar and things don't look so rosy, unless you can take advantage of a special offer. Catching a ferry across the Channel before joining the rail network will virtually halve the cost but will double the journey time.

Bilbao is linked by train with the rest of Spain by **RENFE** (www.renfe.es). A train from Madrid to Bilbao takes six to eight hours and costs from €31 one way.

Road

Bus If neither air nor rail travel appeals, it is also possible to get to Bilbao by coach. **Eurolines** (**T** 01582-404511 in the UK, www.gobycoach.com), has a service from London Victoria (via Paris and Bordeaux), departing at 0800 on Monday and Saturday and arriving in Bilbao at 0430 the following morning. The return leaves Bilbao at 0030 on Thursday and Saturday night, getting to London at 1945 the next evening. There's an extra bus in summer. A return costs about £100; concessions available.

Bilbao, San Sebastián and Vitoria are connected with most major Spanish cities by bus. Long-haul services are efficient, fast and cheap but check the journey time when booking, as some services may stop at other towns en route. A bus from Madrid to Bilbao takes four hours 30 minutes and costs about €25 making it cheaper and faster than the train.

Car Unless you're arriving on the car ferry (see below), the main route into the Basque country is the E05/E70/NI motorway that runs down the southwest coast of France, crossing into Spain at Irún, near San Sebastián. It's fairly heavily tolled but worthwhile, compared to the slow, traffic-plagued *rutas nacionales* on these sectors. Several more scenic but much slower routes cross the Pyrenees at various points.

Sea
P&O (**T** 0870-242 4999, www.poportsmouth.com, www.poferries.com) runs a ferry service from Portsmouth to Santurtzi, 13 km from the centre of Bilbao, but in reality it's more of a cruise than a connection. The ship, *Pride of Bilbao*, is the largest ferry operating out of the UK and has several restaurants, a cinema, pool, sauna and casino, none of which comes cheap: expect to pay £400-500 return with a car. It's a two-night trip and cabin accommodation is mandatory. Many passengers don't even bother to get off the boat when they reach Spain. Boats leave Portsmouth at 2045 every three days except during winter, when there are few crossings. The return ferry leaves Bilbao at 1315.

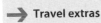 **Travel extras**

Police distinctions There are three main types of police operating in Euskadi. The **Guardia Civil** (green uniform) are a national force responsible for the roads, borders and law enforcement away from towns. They are generally hated by the Basques for their frequent repressionist tactics and torture of prisoners. Not a bunch to get on the wrong side of but civil to tourists. The **Policía Nacional** (brown uniform) are responsible for most urban crimefighting and are the ones to go to if you need to report anything stolen, etc. The **Ertzaintza** are the most dashing force in the region, with cocky red berets. They are a Basque force who deal with day-to-day policing.

Safety The Basque country is an extremely safe place to travel. As everywhere, you should be careful with your belongings but there's no tourist-crime scene here as there is in Barcelona or Madrid. Danger from terrorist or police violence is minimal but steer clear of controversial demonstrations or events. There are dodgy areas in Bilbao: the very sleazy red-light area around Calle San Francisco across the river from the old town is dangerous night and day, and you should avoid the tunnel under the Puente de Arriaga if you're squeamish about needles. San Sebastián and Vitoria are extremely safe unless you get on the wrong end of an argument about football.

Tipping Tipping in Spain is far from compulsory, but much practised. Ten per cent is considered fairly generous in a restaurant, but not excessive; locals tend to tip 5% or less. It's rare for a service charge to be added to a bill. Waiters do not normally expect tips for lunchtime set meals or tapas. In bars and cafés people will often leave small change, especially for table service.

A cheaper and faster option is the service run by **Brittany Ferries** (**T** 08705-561600 in the UK, **T** 942-360 611 in Spain, www.brittanyferries.co.uk) from Plymouth to Santander, 100 km west of Bilbao. Ferries leave the UK on Sunday and Wednesday mornings, taking a shade under 24 hours. Return ferries leave Santander on Monday and Thursday. Prices vary but a reclining seat can usually be had for about £70-90 each way. A car adds at least £140 each way, and cabins start from about £80 for a twin. The service runs year-round, weather permitting. Cheaper offers can sometimes be had at www.ferrysavers.com, **T** 0870-442 4223.

Getting around

Bilbao isn't especially large and is fairly easy to get around on foot: the Guggenheim Museum is about 20 minutes' walk from the old town along the river. To save tired legs, make use of the excellent, modern Metro and tram lines. From Bilbao, the rest of the Basque region is easily accessible by bus from the interurban bus station (Termibus) to the southwest of the centre (Metro and Tram: San Mamés). There are also trains to some destinations.

Bus
Although there's a reasonable network of local buses in Bilbao, they are only useful for a handful of destinations, which are indicated in the text. The majority of interurban buses leave from the **Termibus** station near the football stadium (**T** 944-395077, Metro and Tram: San Mamés). All long-haul destinations are served from here, including **San Sebastián**, with PESA (every 30 mins Mon-Fri, every hr Sat and Sun, 1hr 20mins, €8); and **Vitoria**, with Autobuses La Unión (every 30 mins, 55 mins, €4.80). Note that several smaller Basque towns are served from the bus stops next to Abando train station on Calle Hurtado Amezaga.

Car

Driving in Bilbao can be frustrating, with a complex one-way system, heavy traffic and ambiguous signs. The most convenient places to park are the numerous but expensive underground car parks (€12-20 a day). Metered zones are cheaper but you can't load them up for the whole day. They are indicated by a solid blue line; a dotted blue line marks a zone where there's a time-of-day factor, which will be signposted. If there's no line, it's a free zone but these are few and far between in the centre. There are free car parks near the Begoña basilica and next to Sarriko Metro, beyond Deusto, but these are not especially secure. For paid long-stay parking, follow the signs off Plaza del Ayuntamiento.

Exploring the Basque region by car is relatively easy. Apart from the usual driving hazards, the main nuisances are the tolls on the *autopistas*, which are extortionate. Avoiding these roads often means watching the back of a truck for long stretches on the free but slow *rutas nacionales*. Unleaded petrol costs from €0.90 to €1 per litre.

Cycling

Bilbao isn't especially bicycle-friendly but cycling is a good option for exploring the surrounding countryside. San Sebastián and, in particular, Vitoria are good two-wheel cities, with more planned cycleways and green spots than in busier Bilbao. Getxo is a good area to explore by bicycle, as indeed is most of the Basque coast; the trip between Bilbao and San Sebastián is a particularly rewarding ride, with only a handful of steep sections.

Metro and tram

The newly re-established **tram** network is very handy. There's just one line so far; a scenic one, running from Atxuri station along the river, skirting the Casco Viejo (stopping behind the Teatro Arriaga), then continuing on the other side of the Nervión, stopping at the Guggenheim and the bus station among other places. Trams run every 10 to 15 minutes or so and a single fare costs €1, with ticket machines at the tram stops. Before getting on the tram, you should stamp your ticket in the validation machine on the platform. For further-flung parts of Bilbao, such as the beach or the bus station, the **Metro** is excellent. Modern, fast, efficient and wonderfully spacious, it runs until about midnight Sunday to Thursday, until about 0200 on Friday nights, and all night on Saturdays. A single fare costs €1.15; a day pass is €3. There's one main line running through the city and out to the beach suburbs; a second line will eventually reach the coast on the other side of the estuary.

▸▸ *For a map of the Metro, see the inside front cover.*

Taxi

Taxis are plentiful, both on the street and at cab ranks. If the green light on top is on, they're available. Drivers will only enter the narrow streets of the old town if summoned. Sample fares: from the Casco Viejo to the Guggenheim should cost about €6; Bilbao centre to Getxo, €16; San Sebastián's Parte Vieja to Monte Igueldo, about €8 to the top; Vitoria's train station to the basilica at Armentia, €6 .

Train

Bilbao has three train stations. The main one, **Estación de Abando** (T 902-240202), just across the bridge from the old town, is the terminal of **RENFE**, the national Spanish railway. It's a far from busy network and the bus usually beats it over a given distance but it's the principal mainline service.

Abando is also the main terminus for **Euskotren** (T 902-543210), a handy short-haul train network which connects Bilbao and San Sebastián with many of the smaller Basque towns as well as their own outlying suburbs. The other Bilbao base for these trains is **Estación de Atxuri**, just east of the Casco Viejo.

El Metro

Greater Bilbao was in much need of an efficient public transport network when it commissioned Norman Foster to design an underground Metro system for the city in 1988. In November 1995 the line was opened and the Bilbaínos were impressed with the British architect's work. Foster's design is simple, attractive and, above all, it is spacious, so claustrophobes will be able to banish Bakerloo Line-endured nightmares. Many of the stations are entered through '*fosteritos*', distinctive transparent plastic tubes on the street, named after the architect. The station at Sarriko is dubbed '*El Fosterazo*' for its larger size.

From here, there are trains to San Sebastián, every hour on the hour (2 hrs 39 mins), via Eibar, Durango, Zarautz and Zumaia. It's particularly useful for reaching Euskadi's coastal towns. Gernika is served every hour (53 mins), with trains continuing on to Mundaka and Bermeo.

Finally, narrow-gauge **FEVE** (**T** 944-232266) trains run along the coast to Santander and beyond. They are slow but scenic and leave from the **Estación de Santander** just next to Abando station.

Walking

Much of the charm of the Basque cities is absorbed simply by strolling around. The *paseo*, or *txikiteo*, between 1930 and 2030, is a particularly enjoyable time to be afoot, as everyone takes to the streets with family or friends and simply walks, with not a hint of hurry or destination. In Bilbao, the old town and the riverbank are the focus of the evening *paseo*.

Tours

Specialist tour operators

Amaiur, C General Concha 8, Bilbao, **T** 944-440552,
www.castilloamaiur.com. Cultural and ecological tour specialists.

Euskaltrip, Paseo Colon 17, San Sebastián, **T** 943-290185,
www.euskaltrip.com. Transfers, reservations aswell as cultural
tours of San Sebastián and Euskadi.

Pathfinders, Stita House, 1 Bath Street, Cheltenham,
Gloucestershire GL50 1YE, UK, **T** +44 (0)1242-515712,
www.pathfinders.co.uk. Food and wine tours in the Basque
country and Rioja.

Tenedor, **T/F** 943-313929, www.tenedortours.com.
English-speaking cultural and culinary tours from a
Basque-based company.

Totally Spain, C San Prudencio 29, Edificio Opera, Piso 3º, Oficina
62-B, Vitoria, **T** 945-141538, **T** 0709-229 6272 (in the UK),
www.totallyspain.com. Tours, accommodation and transport.

Walking Connection, 4722 W. Continental Drive, Glendale, AZ
85308, USA, **T**1-602 978 1887, www.walkingconnection.com.
Walking tours of the Basque country.

Sightseeing tours

Bilbao Paso a Paso, **T** 944-730078. Knowledgeable tours of
Bilbao and the whole of Euskadi.

Bisertur, C Gardoki 7, Bilbao, **T** 944-153606, www.bisertur.com. Half-day and day tours of Bilbao and longer regional tours, mainly in Spanish.

San Sebastián A sightseeing bus runs a hop-on, hop-off service along a fixed route of 17 or 25 stops, three times daily on Monday, Wednesday and Thursday, and five times daily from Friday to Sunday. The ticket (€12) is valid for 24 hours. There's also a tourist 'train' (**T** 943-288027), which departs from Teatro Victoria Eugenia every hour. The tourist office can provide self-guided audio tours of the old town, which cost €10.

Guided tours of **Guernika** leave at 1100 from the tourist office, **T** 946-255892.

Boat trips

Barco Pil-Pil, Bilbao, **T** 944-465065. One-hour boat trips are offered on Saturdays and Sundays from April to October, with additional trips Tuesday to Friday in July and August, €9.30 (including drink). Four-hour dinner and dance cruises run all year on Fridays and Saturdays, €49.50; book in advance as the meal is pre-prepared by caterers. The boat leaves from a jetty not far from the Guggenheim Museum.

Euskal Herria Boats run between Getxo and Portugalete via Santurtzi, leaving Getxo hourly on the half hour and Portugalete hourly on the hour. The jaunt across the river mouth takes about 30 minutes.

Barco de Ocio in San Sebastián runs 30-minute trips around the bay, every hour on Saturday and Sunday, €5.50. Boats depart from halfway along aquarium wharf.

Tourist information

Bilbao

Bilbao Turismo (Pl Arriaga s/n, **T** 944-795760, www.bilbao.net; *Mon-Sat 0930-1400, 1600-1930, Sun 0930-1400*), Bilbao's main tourist office, has temporarily moved to the Teatro Arriaga on the edge of the old town. There's also an office at the airport, another in the new town (Pl Ensanche 11; *Mon-Fri 0900-1400, 1600-1930*) and a smaller office by the Guggenheim Museum (Abandoibarra Etorbidea 2; *Tue-Fri 1100-1430, 1530-1800, Sat 1100-1500, 1600-1900, Sun 1100-1400; Jul and Aug Mon-Sat 1000-1500, 1600-1900, Sun 1000-1500*). These offices can provide a good free map of the city; they can also sell you the **Bilbao Card**, which entitles the holder to free transport on local buses, Metro, tram and the Artxanda funicular, as well as providing discounts in several shops and museums. It costs €6 for a day or €12 for three days.

El País Vasco

All tourist offices in Euskadi have an excellent range of material and also have comprehensive maps on sale for €2-3. The efficient, English-speaking office in **San Sebastián** (C Reina Regente 3, **T** 943-481166, **F** 943-481172, www.sansebastianturismo.com; *Mon-Sat 0900-1330, 1530-1900 or until 2000 in summer, Sun 1000-1400*) is busy but helpful. There is also a new tourist office in **Vitoria** (Pl General Loma 1, near the Pl de España, **T** 945-161598, turismo@vitoria-gasteiz.org; *Mon-Sat 1000-1900, Sun 1100-1400.*)

Casco Viejo 33
Bilbao's old quarter is the most charming part of town, a lively jumble of pedestrian streets that has always been the city's social focus.

Riverbank 38
The Nervión riverbank has been and continues to be the focus of most of Bilbao's beautification schemes. Tourists flock to Gehry's Guggenheim, the most emblematic symbol of Bilbao's rejuvenation.

El Ensanche 49
The elegant new town, where sleek tower blocks flank designer shops and hip bars along leafy avenues.

Deusto/Deustu 53
The university district, historically a separate parish, still feels like a town in its own right and has an alternative vibe.

Getxo and around 55
At the mouth of the Nervión, Bilbao's beach suburbs make a great day trip, as they're all easily connected by Metro with the city.

★ Casco Viejo

Tucked into a bend in the river, Bilbao's old town has something of the medina about it; on your first few forays you certainly won't end up where you might have thought you were going. The parallel Siete Calles (Seven Streets) are the oldest part of town, where even the locals struggle to sort out which bar is on which street. There aren't a huge number of sights per se, but there are dozens of quirky shops and some very attractive architecture, so leisurely wandering is the order of the day. The true soul of the the old town emerges in the early evening, however, when Bilbaínos descend on the Casco like bees returning to the hive, strolling the streets, listening to buskers, debating the quality of the pintxos in the myriad bars and sipping wine in the setting sun.

▶▶ *See Sleeping p125, Eating and drinking p152, Bars and clubs p181*

Siete Calles
Metro: Casco Viejo, Tram: Ribera. Map 5, E3, p256

In 1300 the lord of the province of Vizcaya, Don Diego López de Haro V, saw the potential of the fishing village of Bilbao and granted it permission to become a town. By the end of the 14th century the town had three parallel streets running down to the River Nervión: Somera, Artekale and Tendería (street of shopkeepers). Belostikale, Carnicería Vieja, Barrenkale and Barrenkale Barrena were soon added to make up the Siete Calles, the seven original streets of the city. The fledgling town encompassing these streets was walled but, at the end of the 15th century, the original fortifications came down and the city began to grow.

! Bilbao city's coat of arms features two wolves. These are the symbol of Don Diego López, whose family name derives from the Latin for wolf, *lupus*.

The Siete Calles today bristle with bars and shops. Somera is a particularly interesting street, with an alternative feel about it and proudly Basque watering holes. Barrenkale has a well-deserved reputation for boisterous bars!

Catedral de Santiago

Pl Santiago. *Tue-Sat 1000-1300, 1600-1900, Sun 1030-1330, free. Metro: Casco Viejo. Map 5, E3, p256*

In the centre of the Casco Viejo is the Catedral de Santiago, whose slender spire rises high above the tightly packed streets. A graceful Gothic affair, it was mostly built in the late 14th century on the site of a previous church but was devastated by fire in the 1500s and lost much of its original character. Two of its best features are later additions: an arched southern porch and a small but harmonious cloister (if it's locked, try to find an attendant to open it); the small interior has an inclusive, democratic air. The beautifully worked Gothic tomb in the chapel of San Antón is also worth a look. The building became a cathedral in 1950 and has benefited from recent restoration work. A few shops are charmingly nestled into its flank.

Plaza Nueva

Metro: Casco Viejo. Map 5, C2, p256

The 'new' square was finished in 1849 and is one of several cloister-like squares in Euskadi. Described by Unamuno as "my cold and uniform Plaza Nueva", it will particularly appeal to lovers of geometry and symmetry, with its courtly, neo-classical arches. These arches conceal an excellent selection of restaurants and bars, with some of the best *pintxos* in town on offer. In good weather, most have seating outside in the square. In the past, the centre of the square has been ornamented by a statue, a bandstand and, most recently, a fountain but it was cleared for the construction of the underground car park. It comes to life on Sundays, however, for the

We arrived at Bilbao.
After two years and seven months I return to you,
cursed city and city locked deep in my heart…
City ever closer, ever harsher, ever rustier,
ever more cherished.
Bilbao.

Blas de Otero

flea market. At Hallowe'en, the square is a riot of colour, with thousands of floral wreaths on sale for All Saints' Day.

Museo Vasco

Pl Miguel de Unamuno 4, **T** 944-155423. *Tue-Sat 1100-1700, Sun 1100-1400. €3, free on Thu. Metro: Casco Viejo. Map 5, D4, p256*

Attractively set around an old Jesuit college, this museum houses an interesting if higgledy-piggledy series of Basque artefacts and exhibits covering thousands of years. There's a fascinating room-sized relief model of Vizcaya on the top floor, a piece of one of the Gernika oak trees and some good displays on Basque fishing, as well as a decent but poorly presented series of prehistoric finds. Descriptions are currently in Euskara and Spanish only, although English panels are being mooted. The museum's centrepiece is the boarlike *Mikeldi*, of uncertain prehistoric origin.

The slightly shabby plaza, named after the great Bilbao poet and philosopher Miguel de Unamuno, gets very rowdy indeed on Saturday nights, when it's the gathering place for crowds of underage drinkers. Unamuno himself was born in a house on nearby Calle Ronda: a defaced plaque is the only evidence.

Basílica de Begoña

Begoña s/n. *Buses 3 and 30 from Pl Circular, Bus 41 from Gran Vía. Metro: Casco Viejo (take the Begoña/Mallona exit) or the lift from C Esperanza (€0.25), at street level, bear right, then turn right up C Virgen de Begoña. Map 5, A6, p256*

Atop a steep hill above the Casco Viejo is Bilbao's most important church, home of Vizcaya's patron the Virgin of Begoña. It's built in Gothic style on the site of a chapel where the Virgin is said to have appeared in former times. The 13th-century idol occupies a niche in the central *retablo*. The cloister is a later addition, as is the flamboyant tower, which gives a slightly unbalanced feel to the

The philosopher's last stand

One of Bilbao's most famous sons was Miguel de Unamuno, philosophe, academic and poet, who was born in 1864 on Calle Ronda. One of the 'Generation of '98', a new wave of artists and thinkers emerging after the Spanish-American war of 1898, Unamuno was a humanist and a catholic with an idealistic love of truth; making him enemies in a Spain where political beliefs tended to come first. Many Basques have mixed feelings about 'Don Miguel', who, was proud of being Basque but wasn't pro-independence.

When the Civil War broke out, Unamuno, previously a deputy in the Republic, at first supported the uprising in Salamanca, but grew more and more alarmed with the nature of the Nationalist movement.

On 12 October, 1936 he presided as rector at the university's Columbus Day ceremony, which rapidly degenerated into fascist propaganda. A professor denounced Basque and Catalan nationalism as cancers that fascism would cut out. He was followed by General Millán Astray, a war veteran with one eye, one arm and missing fingers, who spoke to a hall resounding to the popular Falangist slogan "long live death". Finally, Unamuno rose to close the meeting. "At times to be silent is to lie", he said. "I want to comment on the speech – to give it that name – of the professor. Let's ignore the personal affront implied. I am a Basque from Bilbao. The bishop (pro-fascist) next to me is Catalan, from Barcelona". He then harshly criticized Astray, who responded by crying "Death to intellectuals". Guns were pointed at the 72 year old, who went on: "You will win, because you have the brute force. But you will not convince. For to convince, you would need what you lack: reason and right in the struggle". Under house arrest, he died a couple of months later, it was said, of a broken heart.

building. Within the basilica is the painting *La Coronación Canónica de la Virgen de Begoña*, an impressive work by the 19th-century Basque painter known as 'Echena', and paintings by Giordano.

From the Casco Viejo, take the lift from Calle Esperanza to Mallona (or leave the Casco Viejo Metro station by the Mallona exit). From there, walk up the hill to the basilica. The park on your left is **Etxebarria**, formerly a factory complex. One of the chimneys has been left for good measure. There are excellent views of the town from here but you can ascend further, behind the basilica, for even better ones out to the sea. On your descent, rather than taking the Mallona lift, head down the flight of stairs next to it; a charming decent into the Casco Viejo warren, emerging on Plaza Unamuno.

Museo Diocesano de Arte Sacro

Pl de la Encarnación 9, **T** 944-320125. *Tue-Sat 1030-1330, 1600-1900, Sun 1030-1330. €2, free on Thu. Metro: Casco Viejo, Tram: Atxuri. Map 5, E6, p256*

On a lovely cobbled square, this museum, set in a former monastery, features an attractive sunken cloister. The wide-ranging collection deals in a millennium's worth of religious art and artefacts, mostly taken from churches around Vizcaya. While many feel that the works would be better left *in situ*, it is worth remembering how difficult it is to maintain and protect valuable artworks in near-deserted areas. The art ranges from high quality to overly sentimentalized.

Riverbank

The Nervión river made Bilbao, and Bilbao almost killed the Nervión: until quite recently, pollution levels were sky-high. Although your immune system would still object to you taking a dip, the change in the river is noticeable. If you only take one stroll in Bilbao, an evening paseo from the Casco Viejo along the river to the Guggenheim should be it. The tram is another good way to see the river, running more or less along its banks west from Atxuri station to the Guggenheim and Euskalduna Palace. The sights below follow this order.

▸▸ *See Sleeping p128, Eating and drinking p155, Bars and clubs p181*

Mercado de la Ribera

C Ribera s/n, **T** 944-157086. *Metro: Casco Viejo, Tram: Ribera. Map 5, F3, p256*

Built on the site where stallholders used to come for the weekly market, this art deco riverside building is a permanent market of ample size. With over 400 stalls of fruit, veggies, meat and fish spread over three floors, it's the major centre for fresh produce in Bilbao. Come in the morning if you want to get the true flavour; the afternoons are comparatively quiet. Skip the meat floor if you don't want to see pigs' heads and horse butchers!

Teatro Arriaga

Pl del Arriaga 1, **T** 944-792036. *Metro: Casco Viejo, Tram: Arriaga. Map 5, D1, p256*

This large and ornate building sits just outside the Casco Viejo on its own block. It dominates the surrounding area and seems very sure of itself but was, in fact, only reopened in 1986, after decades of neglect. Originally opened in 1890, with miraculous new electric lighting, it was largely destroyed by a fire in 1915. The theatre has been restored in plush *fin de siècle* style, with chandeliers and sweeping staircases, and, at times, presents some cutting-edge art. The theatre is named after Juan Crisóstomo de Arriaga, a Bilbaíno boy who was inevitably nicknamed the 'Spanish Mozart' when he started dashing off octets before hitting puberty. He perished even younger than Mozart, dying in Paris in 1826, 10 days short of his 20th birthday.

Café Boulevard
C Arenal 3, **T** 944-153128. *Metro: Casco Viejo. Map 5, D2, p256*

Fans of art deco will not want to miss this refurbished defender
of the style, unchanged since the early 20th century, when it was
Bilbao's beloved meeting place. Founded in 1871, it declined in
parallel with the Teatro Arriaga opposite. Rejuvenated, it's now as
vibrant as it was in the days of Unamuno, when earnest discussions
in cafés fuelled the arts world.

El Arenal
Metro: Casco Viejo, Tram: Arriaga. Map 5, C1, p256

Between the old town and the Nervión, this park area is a focus of
Bilbao community life: a busy nexus point for strollers, lovers,
demonstrators and dog walkers. Formerly an area of marshy sand,
it was drained in the 18th century. There's a bandstand with
frequent performances, often of folk dancing. From here, the
Puente del Arenal crosses the Nervión to the new town.

San Nicolás de Bari
C Arenal s/n. *Metro: Casco Viejo. Map 5, C2, p256*

The baroque façade of this 18th-century church dominates the
Parque del Arenal and is attractive when sunlit. When Bilbao was
a village, this was the fishermen's quarter, with a tiny chapel
dedicated to Nicolás, patron saint of sailors. As Bilbao grew,
the chapel was replaced by a larger church, which remained half
finished for more than two centuries before being demolished.
The current church is spacious but fairly uninteresting.

● *Behind the church of St Nicholas, on grimy Calle Esperanza, is
a* frontón *where there are frequent games of* pelota, *both organized
and informal.*

You are, Nervión, the history of the town,
you her past and her future, you are memory
always becoming hope.

Miguel de Unamuno

Ayuntamiento

Pl Ernesto Erkoreka. *Metro: Casco Viejo, Tram: Ayuntamiento.*
Map 4, A11, p255

The Ayuntamiento, or town hall, was built in 1892 and is an
example of the new baroque that, along with art nouveau, was a
reaction to the stifling artistic atmosphere that had prevailed in
Spain for over a century. It's topped by a quirky little spire that's a
bit out of place. It was designed by Joaquín de Rucoba, who was
also responsible for the Teatro Arriaga.

In front, by the river, is an intriguing sculpture by the
controversial late artist Jorge Oteiza. The evocative rusted-iron
work, entitled *Ovoide de la Desocupación de la Esfera*, has been
nicknamed *la txapela* ('the beret') by locals. Created in 1958, it
was only recently installed here.

★ Zubizuri footbridge

Between Paseo Campo de Volantín and C de Marina.
Tram: Uribitarte. Map 4, A8, p255

Santiago Calatrava's bridges have won him world renown and this
is among his most graceful. Inaugurated in 1994, it was a powerful
symbol of Bilbao's renewal before the Guggenheim was close to
completion. Shining white in the sun like the ribs of some marine
creatures, it seems impossibly light. Although the footway is made
of glass, the Bilbao authorities have controversially covered it in
non-slip plastic which blocks the view down to the water but
prevents the less sure-of-foot from slipping into the river. The
funky name means 'white bridge' in Euskara.

Funicular to Monte Artxanda

From Pl Funicular. *Mon-Sat 0715-2200, Sun 0815-2200 (until 2300 in
summer). €0.78. Map 3, A1, p252*

In a city enclosed by hills, there are sure to be some good vistas on offer and one of the best is from the top of Monte Artxanda. Not far from the Zubizuri, a bright-red funicular rises to the top, a popular weekend gathering place for the burghers of Bilbao. There are a couple of places to eat but, if the day is nice, a picnic is called for.

Paseo Uribitarte
Map 4, B7-11, p254

This long riverside walk leading to the Guggenheim Museum is where Bilbaínos gather for the evening stroll, or *paseo*. Although the Nervión occasionally has problems with personal hygiene, Uribitarte is a lovely promenade, which sometimes seems like the parade ground at a dog show as some seriously pampered pooches are brought out to take the city air.

★ Guggenheim Museum
Abandoibarra Etorbidea 2, **T** 944-359000, www.guggenheim-bilbao.es *Tue-Sun 1000-2000, plus Mon 1000-2000 in Jul and Aug. €10, students/pensioners €6, under-12s free, €11 including Museo de Bellas Artes. Free guided tours 1130, 1230, 1630, 1830 (Spanish, English and Euskara depending on demand), audio tour €3.50. Tram: Guggenheim, Metro: Moyúa, Buses 13, 27, 38, 46, 48 stop a block away on Alameda Recalde. Map 4, B6, p254*

More than anything else, it is this building that has thrust Bilbao so firmly back on to the world stage. Daring in concept and brilliant in execution, it has driven a massive boom in the local confidence as well as, more prosaically, in the economy. Its success has given the green light to further ambitious transformation of formerly industrialized parts of the city.

It all started when the Guggenheim Foundation, strapped for cash (or something like that…), decided to build a new museum to

Titanium titan
Frank Gehry's Guggenheim dominates the regenerated riverfront in the centre of Bilbao.

enable more of its collection to be exhibited. Many cities around the globe were considered but the Basque government was prepared to foot the US$100 million bill for its construction.

Frank Gehry won the design competition and created a shining temple of a building that completely fulfils the maxim of 'architecture as art'. As he later commented: "the idea was that the building had to be able to accommodate the biggest and heaviest of contemporary sculpture on the one hand, and a Picasso drawing on the other hand. In the first sketch I put a bunch of principles down, then I become self-critical of those images and those principles, and that evokes the next set of responses… and those evolve, and at some point I stop, because that's it." His masterstroke was to use titanium, an expensive soft metal normally reserved for aeroplanes and the like. Gehry was intrigued by its futuristic sheen and malleable qualities. The panels of titanium are literally paper-thin and make the building shimmer, giving the impression that the architect has managed to capture motion. The exuberant curves recall the shape of a fish, one of Gehry's favourite motifs, and the structure as a whole could almost be a writhing school of herring or salmon.

One of the most impressive features of the design is the way it interacts with the city. Crossing a street in the centre of town, you can look up and see the Guggenheim, framed by older buildings, like some unearthly vehicle that's just landed. Gehry had to contend with the ugly bulk of the Puente de la Salve running through the middle of his site, yet managed to incorporate the bridge into his plans. The raised tower at the museum's eastern end has no purpose other than to link the building more effectively with the town upriver; it works.

The building also interacts fluidly with the river itself: the pool at the museum's feet almost seems part of the Nervión, and Fuyiko Nakaya's mist sculpture, when turned on, further blurs the boundaries between nature and art. This artwork is entitled *FOG*, which also happens to be the architect's initials.

A couple of creatures have escaped the confines of the gallery and live in the open air. Jeff Koons' giant floral sculpture, *Puppy*, sits eagerly greeting visitors. Originally a touring attraction that visited the city for the opening of the museum in 1997, he couldn't escape the clutches of the kitsch-hungry Bilbaínos, who demanded that he stayed put. On the other side of the building, a sinister spider-like creature guards the waterside approach. Entitled *Maman*, we can only be thankful that sculptor Louise Bourgeois' mother had long since passed away when it was created. It's a striking piece of work, and a bizarre sight when shrouded in mist. On the western side of the building is *Quantum Field-X*, two huge cube-like structures covered in panels onto which coloured laser beams are projected.

What about the inside? It is, after all, an art museum. Gehry's idea was that there would be two types of gallery. "galleries for dead artists, which have classical [square or rectangular] shapes, and galleries for living artists, which have funny shapes, because they can fight back". The embodiment of the latter is Gallery 104, built with the realization that many modern artworks were too big for traditional museums. Central to this space is Richard Serra's *Snake*, whose curved iron sheets will carry whispers from one end to the other. A hundred feet long and weighing 180 tons, *Snake* is an interactive piece – walk through it, talk through it, touch it. This, however, is one of only a few permanent works to live in the museum; the rest are temporary visitors, some taken from the permanent collection of the Guggenheim Foundation, others appearing in a range of exhibitions.

Architecturally, the interior is a very soothing space with natural light flooding into the atrium and three floors of galleries radiating off the central space. Jenny Holzer's *Installation for Bilbao* is an arresting nine-column LED display, uniting the different levels of the building and creating a torrent of primal human sentiment expressed simply in three languages. There's also a space reserved for Picasso's *Guernica*, which the Basque government has persistently but so far unsuccessfully tried to prise away from Madrid's Reina Sofía gallery.

For a look at smaller-scale Gehry work, drop into the reading room on the ground floor, furnished with his unique cardboard chairs and tables. The café also has chairs designed by him. The museum has an excellent modern art bookshop and a souvenir shop.

Palacio Euskalduna

C Abandoibarra 4, **T** 944-310310. *Tram: Euskalduna, Metro: San Mamés. Map 4, F3, p254*

Opened in 1998 on the site of the last Bilbao shipyard, this bizarre building echoes both shipbuilding and Vizcaya's iron trade, with its rust-coloured bulk looming over the river. Awkwardly situated, hemmed in by a busy bypass, the structure leaves many people cold, although it is impressive in a clumsy kind of way. Particularly interesting are the coathanger 'trees' at the front. It's now a major venue for conferences and concerts, particularly classical.

Museo Marítimo Ría de Bilbao

Muelle Ramón de la Sota 1, **T** 902-131000, www.museomaritimo bilbao.org. *Tue-Fri 1000-1400, 1600-1800, Sat and Sun 1000-1400, 1600-2000. €4 (extra for special exhibitions). Tram: Euskalduna, Metro: San Mamés. Map 4, G2, p254*

This new museum nestles under the Euskalduna covered bridge, which sweeps into Deustu in a confident curve. It occupies the site of what was once an important shipbuilding and cargo area and it examines the maritime history of this proud city. A massive derrick and various ships in dry dock are part of the outside exhibition, while, inside, the focus is on the Bilbao estuary and Vizcayan shipping in general. It's dry but fascinating, with a couple of good audio-visual presentations in English (other displays have translation sheets). One of the highlights is the aerial photograph of Bilbao and its *ría*. There are often excellent temporary exhibitions, which have included visiting 'guest ships' that moor outside.

El Ensanche

The residents of old Bilbao had long been crammed into the small Casco Viejo area when the boom came and the population began to surge. In 1876 the Plan de Ensanche (expansion) de Bilbao was approved and the area across the river from the old town was divided up into segments, governed by the curve of the Nervión. The design drew on classical and Renaissance models, with a large elliptical plaza intended as the hub of the new zone. The Ensanche soon became Bilbao's business district and, today, its graceful avenues are lined with stately office buildings, prestigious shops and more than a few bars.

▸▸ *See Sleeping p130, Eating and drinking p155, Bars and clubs p181*

Plaza Circular
Metro: Abando, Tram: Casino. Map 4, C11, p255

Also called Plaza España (but not by many Basques!), this is a busy focus of new town goings-on. Bilbao's founder, Don Diego López de Haro, stands on a monument in the centre, although he certainly wouldn't recognize his sleepy fishing village anymore. Behind him looms the massive building of the Banco de Bilbao y Vizcaya, a skyscraper with windows tinted in a colour that seems permanently to reflect the setting sun, even when it rains. The main railway station, Abando, is just off the plaza, which is busy at all hours. One of Bilbao's most characterful cafés, La Granja, is on the north side; a good place for evening drinks and snacks.

Gran Vía Don Diego López de Haro
Metro: Moyúa, Abando, Tram: Casino. Map 4, D10, p255

Named after the founder of the city and spanning the entire Ensanche, Bilbao's principal street starts at Plaza Circular and is lined with banks and other important buildings, including the Palacio Foral, the seat of the Vizcayan government. There are many good examples of late 19th-century architecture; their imposing and sober bulk seems to define the work ethic that drove Bilbao's industrial boom. It's also a key shopping street with the massive El Corte Inglés at one end and a number of other boutiques along its length.

Jardines de Albia
Metro: Abando. Map 4, C10, p255

A small, peaceful park in the heart of the business district, this is where employees of the adjacent law courts come to wind down. The headquarters of the PNV (Basque Nationalist Party) also face the gardens. There's a statue of the writer Antonio de Trueba at one end. He wrote poems, history and stories in a simple nostalgic style, very popular with his 19th-century public and with Queen Isabella II.

Plaza Moyúa
Metro: Moyúa. Map 4, E8, p255

When the Ensanche was planned, the central focus was to be a plaza of oval shape. The result was this busy meeting of eight streets, sometimes known as 'Elíptica', around a French-style formal garden. The plaza is overlooked by the grand old **Hotel Carlton**, where Ernest Hemingway and a multitude of other celebrities used to lay their heads. It was the headquarters of the republican Basque government during the Civil War, before it was forced into exile after the surrender of the city. Another interesting building is the spiky modernist **Palacio Chávarri**, which is used by the government.

Museo de Bellas Artes de Bilbao

Pl del Museo 2, **T** 944-396060, www.museobilbao.com. *Tue-Sat 1000-2000, Sun 1000-1400. €4.50 or €11 with Guggenheim permanent collections, €2 audio guide. Metro: Moyúa, Tram: Abandoibarra. Map 4, E6, p254*

Not wishing to be outdone by its titanium colleague, the Museo de Bellas Artes has tried to keep up with the times by adding a modern building of its own to the existing museum. The result is a harmonious credit to its architect, Luís Uriarte, who seamlessly and attractively fused new to old. The collection is a medley of modern (mostly Basque) art and older works; there's also a new space for temporary exhibitions. The late Basque sculptors Eduardo Chillida and Jorge Otelza are well represented. In addition to avant-garde multimedia work by young artists. Among the portraits, the jutting jaw of the Habsburg kings is visible in two famous works. The first, of a young Philip II, is by the Dutchman Moro; the second, a portrait of Philip IV, attributed to Velasquéz, and similar to his representation of the same king in the Prado, is a masterwork. The decline of Spain can be seen in the sad king's haunted but intelligent eyes, which seem to follow the viewer around the room. A lighter note is (perhaps unintentionally) struck by the anonymous *Temptations of St Anthony*, which shows the saint being pestered by a trio of colourful demons.

Parque de Doña Casilda de Iturrizar

Metro: Moyúa, Tram: Euskalduna. Map 4, E5, p254

This wedge-shaped park provides a big dose of greenery to central Bilbao. It's a pretty, if slightly tired, retreat for a walk or a doze in the sun. The fountain, surrounded by a very pretty colonnade draped with wisteria, is a tranquil spot which occasionally hosts open-air concerts in summer. Below, in the park's centre, is a pond with a desultory collection of depressed peacocks and waterfowl. On clement weekends the park fills with roaming families.

Calle Ercilla and Plaza Indautxu

Metro: Moyúa, Indautxu. Map 4, H7, p255

The pedestrianized part of Calle Ercilla tracks southwest from Plaza Moyúa and is yet another favoured spot for the *paseo*. It's one of Bilbao's premier shopping streets, with several high-class boutiques. The street ends at Plaza Indautxu, centre of the district of the same name, which is well stocked with bars.

Plaza de Toros de Vista Alegre

C Martin Agüero 1, **T** 944-448698, **F** 944-102564, www.torosbilbao.com. *Museum Mon-Fri 1030-1300, 1600-1800. €1.20. Metro: Indautxu. Map 3, G6, p252*

Bilbao's temple to bullfighting sees most action during Semana Grande in August, when there are *corridas* all week. The locals are knowledgeable and demanding of their matadors, and the bulls they face are acknowledged to be among the most *bravo* in Spain. Tickets to the spectacle don't come cheap, starting at about €30. Check the website for details of *corridas* and ticketing. The bullring also houses a museum dedicated to tauromachy; there are displays on the history of the practice, as well as memorabilia of famous matadors and bulls. It's one of the few museums open on a Monday, but it's closed at weekends. The ring also hosts occasional concerts.

San Mamés

C Felipe Serrate s/n, **T** 944-411445, www.athletic-club.net. *Museum: Mon-Fri 1030-1330, 1600-1900, Sat 1000-1400, 1600-1900, Sun 1000-1400. €6. Metro: San Mamés, Tram: San Mamés. Map 3, F2, p252*

There are few football teams in the world with the social and political significance of Athletic Bilbao (see p213). Support for the team is a religion and this, their home stadium, is known as the 'Cathedral of

Best

★ Alternatives to the Guggenheim

- Walking to the old town from the Basílica de Begoña, p36.
- Visiting the Museo de Bellas Artes, p51.
- Attending an Athletic Bilbao home game, p52.
- Crossing the estuary on the Puente Vizcaya, p58.
- Eating *pintxos* in the Casco Viejo, p151.

Football'. Services are held fortnightly, usually on Sundays at about 1700. Tickets for games generally go on sale at the ground two days before and the Monday papers frequently devote ten pages or more to Athletic's game. It's well worth going to one of the matches, which are far more friendly, social affairs than the average match in the rest of Europe. The Basque crowd is fervent but good-natured. Visiting fans from Spanish clubs will frequently try to wind up the local supporters by provocatively waving Spanish flags; in response, the home fans usually burst into a gleeful chant of "*Españoles: hijos de puta*", suggesting that Spanish mothers have a very old profession. This is an example of the Spanish football tradition of *morbo*, or the provocative rivalry between fans.

The ground also holds a small museum, displaying trophies and other memorabilia of 'Los Leones'. Admission includes a guided tour of the ground.

Deusto/Deustu

On the right bank of the Nervión, just across the river from the Guggenheim and the Euskalduna concert hall, is the university barrio de Deusto (recently officially renamed Deustu). Traditionally frequented by artists, students and agitators, the cafés and bars hum with political discussion.

▸▸ *See Sleeping p132, Eating and drinking p161, Bars and clubs p181*

Universidad de Deusto

Av de las Universidades 24, **T** 944-139000, **F** 944-139098.
Metro: Deustu.   Map 4, B4, p254

Bilbao's principal university was founded in 1886 by Jesuits as
Basque centre of learning and played an important role in Basque
nationalism. After the Civil War, Franco banned public universities in
the Basque country, fearing they would breed opposition, but
Deusto remained, privately run by the Jesuits, and became an
important centre of radical opposition. Texts and music written in
the Euskara language, outlawed by Franco, circulated clandestinely
on campus, and illegal lessons were given outside of class time. With
a high academic standard, it now has over 20,000 students and staff.
● *The refined neo-classical main building, slightly downstream
from the Guggenheim, is the place to come for a postcard-perfect
snap of Frank Gehry's masterpiece, particularly in the evening light.*

El Tigre

C Ribera Botica Vieja 23.   *Metro: Deustu, Tram: Euskalduna.*
Map 4, E2, p254

One of Bilbao's most distinctive buildings, this was originally built
as a pavilion to house the small workshops of local tradespeople. It
was the first and remains the most impressive of its kind, though
there are some others still in operation along the Deusto riverbank.
Topped with a huge stone lion but perversely named El Tigre (the
tiger), the building has recently been converted into luxury
apartments, as Deusto inevitably becomes trendy.

Iglesia de San Pedro de Deusto

Pl de San Pedro. *Metro: Deustu. Map 4, D1, p254*

This 500-year-old building, in late Gothic style, is the parish church
of Deusto. Despite its modern additions, this is a good example of

a traditional Basque church, with its high triple nave and simple bell tower. The competent *retablo* depicting the life of St Peter is a Renaissance work by two Basque Martíns, Basabe and Ruíz.

Getxo and around

At the mouth of the Nervión, 20 km or so from Bilbao, is the fashionable barrio of Getxo. Very much a separate town rather than a suburb, Getxo is a wealthy, sprawling district encompassing the eastern side of the estuary, a couple of beaches, attractive stately mansions, a modern marina and an old harbour, surrounded by a tiny but oh-so-pretty whitewashed village . There's a very relaxed feel about the place, perhaps born of a combination of the healthy seaside air and a lack of anxiety about where the next meal's coming from. Getxo is linked by the improbably massive Puente Vizcaya with the grittier town of Portugalete, in its day a flourishing medieval port and a traditional port workers' suburb. Not far from Getxo stretch the languid beach suburbs of Sopelana, Plentzia and Gorliz; great stopovers, with plenty of restaurants and good hotels and campsites.
▸▸ *See Sleeping p133, Eating and drinking p162*

Metro: Areeta, Gobela, Neguri, Aiboa, Algorta and Bidezabal. Buses 3411 and 3413 run from Pl Moyúa every 30 mins.

Playa de Ereagat
Metro: Neguri.

Ereagat is Getxo's principal stretch of sand and the location of the town's finer hotels and general seaside life. In truth, it's an inferior beach: most of the view is taken up by the dockyards across the estuary, while the distinctly black-tinged sand keeps many people back on the promenade. Still, it's an important social scene, and you haven't been to Getxo if you haven't strolled along its length, taking a coffee at one of the hotels.

Walking through Getxo

Distance: 3 km
Sturdy shoes required.

Start from **San Nicolás de
Bari** and head downhill along
the pedestrian street Calle
Basagoiti, making a detour
(if you're in the mood) to the
shopping areas to your left
around Calle Telletxe. After
briefly joining the main road,
the pedestrian stretch continues
downhill. It's a pretty avenue
lined with what were once
very swish mansions. One of
the most striking is **Casa
Rosada** (pink house), which
no doubt won more accolades
for its architecture than its name.
At the end is the pointy **Iglesia
de San Ignacio**, behind
which stands the sturdier
Ayuntamiento (town hall),
built of Berango sandstone
and featuring spirited Moorish
ornamentation under its eaves.
Descending the main road,
Algortako Etorbidea, take
the steep right down Calle
Ereagako Jaispidea and turn left
when you reach the beach.

Rounding the headland past
the marina, you come to **Casa
de Náufragos**, built over the
sea on arches, while on the
landward side is a series of
ostentatious 20th-century
palacios. Follow the water along
a lengthy promenade until you
reach the **monument to
Churruca**, and a landscaped
mole stretching into the estuary.
Churruca was the engineer who
channelled out this part of the
waterway in the 19th century,
making Bilbao accessible to large
vessels; a vital step in its growth.
The monument is in classic
heroism-of-the-workers style:
the engineer serenely watches
two figures seemingly trying to
crush each other under a slab of
stone, symbolizing the struggle
between earth and water. Pass
the hulking, modern **Iglesia
de Nuestra Señora de las
Mercedes** (which contains
highly-regarded frescoes) to
reach the unmistakeable form
of the **Puente Vizcaya** and
the popular shopping area of
Las Arenas (Areeta).

Whitewashed houses line the streets around the Puerto Viejo and give Getxo a Mediterranean feel.

Puerto Viejo
Metro: Algorta.

The tiny harbour, now silted up, is a reminder of the days when Getxo made its living from fish. It is overlooked by solemn statues of a fisherman and a *sardinera*, perhaps mystified at the lack of boats. Perching above, a densely packed knot of white houses and narrow lanes gives the little village a very Mediterranean feel, unless the *sirimiri*, the Bilbao drizzle, has put in an appearance. There are a couple of restaurants and bars in which to soak up the ambience of this area, which is Getxo's prettiest quarter.

San Nicolás de Bari
Metro: Algorta.

At the top of the old port stands this attractive church. The stone is warm and rough-cut, making it a building that you want to touch. A cool verandah runs around it and there's a porch facing the square, which is used for impromptu *pelota* games by young locals. The church was built in the mid-19th century and is an appealing example of neo-classicism in the Basque country.

Playa de Arrigunaga
Metro: Bidezabal

Far more inviting than Getxo's main beach, this one faces out to sea and hence avoids the estuary's pollution. Flanked by crumbly cliffs, it's got a more secluded feel too (except at weekends). On top of the cliff to the right is a surprising sight – an attractive 18th-century windmill in tip-top condition. The beach is less protected than Ereaga, so on some days the windmill has a better time of it than the shivering bathers.

Puente Vizcaya
T 944-638854, www.puente-colgante.com. *Daily 1000-sunset.* €*0.25 per person,* €*1.05 per car, walkway* €*3. Metro: Areeta.*

A bizarre cross between a bridge and a ferry, the Puente Vizcaya, or Puente Colgante (hanging bridge), was opened in 1893, at a time when large steel structures were *à la mode* in Europe. The challenge was to connect the estuary towns of Getxo and Portugalete without blocking the *ría* to shipping. The solution involved a 'gondola' suspended by cables from a high steel span. It's a fascinating piece of engineering: the modern gondola zooms back and forth, with six cars plus foot passengers aboard. You can also ascend to the walkway 50 m above. While it's not the Eiffel Tower experience the brochure suggests, it does provide good views.

Portugalete

Euskotren from Ahando (Sunturtzi line) every 12 mins Mon-Fri, every 20 mins Sat and Sun, Metro: Areeta (across bridge), Bus 3152 from the Arenal bus station (Mon-Sat).

On the other side of the Puente Vizcaya from Getxo is Portugalete, a solid working-class town with a significant seafaring history. In former times, before Churruca did his channelling work, the Nervión estuary was a silty minefield of shoals, meanders and sandbars, a nightmare to navigate in anything larger than a rowing boat. Thus Bilbao was still a good few hours' journey by boat from the open sea and Portugalete's situation at the mouth of the *ría* gave it great importance as a port. Given its charter by Doña María Díaz de Haro, 'the Kind', it flourished as a whaling town and commercial port. Nowadays, although parts of it look thoroughly functional, it preserves a characterful narrow-streeted old town and attractive waterfront walkway.

Above the waterside, the old *casco* is dominated by the **Iglesia de Santa María**, commissioned by Doña María the Kind at the time of the town's foundation, although the current building, in Gothic style, dates from the early 16th century There's a small museum inside. Next to it, the **Torre de Salazar** is what remains of the formidable compound built by Juan López de Salazar, a major landowner, in about 1380. The main living area was on the second floor, with a prison below. Luís García Salazar, an early chronicler of Vizcaya, spent the last years of his life locked up here by his loving sons. The tower remained occupied until 1934, when a fire evicted the last residents.

Passion flower

"It is better to be the widow of a hero than the wife of a coward".
Dolores Ibárruri

One of the most prominent figures of the Spanish Civil War, Dolores Ibárruri, from the Bilbao suburb of Gallarta, near Portugalete, was known as '*La Pasionaria*' (the passion flower) for her inspirational public speaking.

Formerly a servant and a *sardinera* (sardine seller), she suffered grinding poverty and the loss of two daughters in infancy but rose to prominence in the Communist Party in the 1930s, becoming a deputy in the parliament in 1936. (She was released from prison to take up her post.) When the Civil War broke out, she became a potent symbol of the defence of Madrid and the struggle against Fascism, as well as of empowered womanhood. Straightforward, determined and always dressed in black, she adopted the war cry *"No pasarán"* ("they shall not pass"), which was taken up all over Republican Spain. She was instrumental in the recruitment and morale-building of anti-fascist soldiers, including the International Brigades. When the latter were later withdrawn, she famously thanked them: "You can go proudly. You are history: you are legend. We shall not forget you".

Ibárruri was never much involved in the plotting and infighting that plagued the Republican cause and was able to claim at the end of the war: "I have neither blood nor gold upon my hands". When Franco won in 1939, she fled to Russia and lived in exile in Moscow.

The dictator died in 1975 and, after 38 years in exile, Ibárruri was re-elected to her old seat at the first elections in 1977. On her return to Spain the 82 year-old Pasionaria, still wearing black, proclaimed to a massive crowd: "I said they shall not pass, and they haven't". Dolores Ibárruri died in 1989.

On the other side of the Puente Colgante, the **Muelle de Hierro**, built by Churruca, stretches north into the estuary. It was this breakwater that finally banished the troublesome sandbar that kept forming at the mouth of the estuary and impeded shipping.

The beaches beyond

Metro: Larrabasterra, Sopelana, Plentzia.

Beyond Getxo a series of beaches, accessible by Metro, offer less crowded sunseeking and a variety of watersports and other activities (see p28). **Gorrondatxe** and **Barinatxe**, reached by walking from Larrabasterra Metro, can feature some fairly have-a-go waves, and are the best surfing options on this stretch; the latter is nicknamed 'the wild beach'. Further along, the strands of **Sopelana** and **Plentzia/Gorliz**, both with their own Metro stops not far away, are more sedate, and good for escaping the crowds. Beyond the beach at Gorliz there are decent walks along the jagged coastline.

Castillo Butrón

Barrio Gatika s/n, **T** 946-151110, **F** 946-151525. *Mar-Sep daily 1030-2000; Oct-Feb Mon-Fri 1030-1730, Sat 1100-1800.*

In the hinterlands behind Plentzia is a bizarre sight: the imposing bulk of a castle that would seem more at home in the Scottish Highlands or a Hollywood studio. Although the castle was the family home of the Butróns as far back as the 13th century, today's impressive structure was built in medieval style in the late 1800s. Bristling with turrets and castellated beyond belief, it sits in a woody park signposted off the road between Getxo and Plentzia. Inside, a series of dummies reconstruct medieval life but it doesn't seem dank enough to really call the period to mind.

Listings

⊙ Museums and galleries

Bilbao

- **Guggenheim Museum** The epitome of Bilbao's transformation, p43.
- **Museo de Bellas Artes de Bilbao** Spanish art, p51.
- **Museo Diocesano de Arte Sacro** Religious art set around a lovely cloister, p38.
- **Museo Marítimo Ría de Bilbao** Dry but fascinating museum about Bilbao seafaring and shipbuilding, p48.
- **Museo Vasco** Basque artefacts covering thousands of years of history, p36.

San Sebastián

- **Kutxaespacio de la Ciencia** Interactive science, p95.
- **Museo Chillida-Leku** A great number of works by the late Basque sculptor Eduardo Chillida, p96.
- **Museo de San Telmo** A wide-ranging collection that includes much Basque art, both modern and older, p85.
- **Museo Naval** Basque naval heritage, p82.

Vitoria

- **Artium** An exciting building for modern Basque art, p104.
- **Museo de Arqueología** Archaeological finds, p110.
- **Museo de Bellas Artes** A collection of Basque art, p106.

El País Vasco/Euskadi

- **Museo de la Paz** (Gernika) Moving museum dedicated to peace and to documenting the Gernika atrocity, p70.
- **Museo Ignacio Zuloaga** (Zumaia) Works by Zuloaga, p79.
- **Museo de Simón Bolívar** (Bolibar, near Markina), p76.
- **Museo Zumalacárregui** (Ormaiztegi) The childhood home of Tomás Zumalacárregui, swashbuckling general, p100.

El País Vasco/Euskadi

Basque coastline 65

The rugged coast east of Bilbao has great beaches and appealing fishing towns that historically linked the Basque nation with daring maritime expeditions. Unmissable Gernika is just inland.

San Sebastián/Donostia 80

One of the peninsula's most beautiful cities, San Sebastián has a light and leisurely feel, and draws throngs of holidaymakers in summer.

Around San Sebastián 97

The Basque coast continues east to France, while inland are startlingly green hills interspersed with jagged peaks and quintessentially Basque towns.

Vitoria/Gasteiz 103

While it lacks the metropolitan vitality of Bilbao or the languid beauty of San Sebastián, this is a very satisfying city, much-loved by most who visit it.

Alava/Araba Province 110

The place to come for unspoilt nature, with areas of great natural beauty and plenty of scope for outdoor activities. What's more, some of the finest Riojas are produced in the wineries here.

Basque coastline

The Basque coastline, stretching east from Bilbao to France, is jagged and spectacular, with wave-beaten cliffs topped by green vegetation. There are a number of excellent sandy beaches and several very characterful fishing towns.

East of Bilbao

A brisk half-hour's walk is all that separates the fishing towns of Bermeo and Mundaka but they couldn't be more different. Mundaka is petite and, these days, slightly upmarket, as visitors come to admire its beautiful harbour and mourn its famous wave. Bermeo puts Mundaka in the shade in fishing terms: it's one of the most important ports on this coast and has a good atmosphere and an attractive old town. East of Bermeo, the road heads inland and crosses the protected Oka estuary at Gernika (see p69). On the other side, beyond the beaches at the mouth of the ría, the land becomes rough-edged, with stirring cliffs and startling geological folds contrasting with green foliage. Fishing is god here and some of the small villages are more accessible by sea than by land. The major town, Lekeitio, is one of Euskadi's highlights.

➤➤ *See Sleeping p134, Eating and drinking p164, Bars and clubs p185*

Euskotren runs every hour from Bilbao's Atxuri station to Gernika, Mundaka and Bermeo; there are also buses from C Hurtado Amezaga (alongside Abando station). For other destinations, such as Lekeitio, catch a bus from Bilbao's Termibus terminal. It's a short drive from Bilbao to Bermeo on the BI-631 or to Gernika on the A8/E70 and the BI-635. A pleasant detour is to head from Bilbao to Getxo and then follow the coast through the beach suburbs of Sopelana and Plentzia to Bakio and Bermeo, before cutting inland to Gernika to cross the Oka (Urdaibai) estuary and heading out to the coast again.

Bermeo

35 km northeast of Bilbao via the BI-631. *Train: hourly from Bilbao's Atxuri station. Bus: every 30 mins with Bizkaibus from C de Hurtado Amezaga. Map 6, off A4, inside back cover*

Bermeo is a typical Basque fishing town with a self-sufficient feel. The town was officially founded in the 13th century and had probably been a pioneering whaling settlement for a couple of centuries before that. The ships for Christopher Columbus' second voyage in 1493 were built in Bermeo and many of the sailors were locals. Bermeo's proud maritime history is covered in its **Museo del Pescador** (Pl Torrontero 1, **T** 946-881171, **F** 946-186454; *Tue-Sat 1000-1330, 1600-1930, Sun 1000-1330; free*). Set in a 15th-century tower in the old part of Bermeo, overlooking the harbour, the museum gives a detailed history of all the ports on the Basque coast, displays tools of the fishing trade, discusses the Basque whaling industry and provides information about the various fish that have been caught here through history.

There's still a great deal of action in the fishing harbour, with boats coming and going and jostling for position. There's a big *frontón* for *pelota* by the harbour; Bermeo likes to see itself as Vizcaya's number two sporting city and results sometimes bear this out.

The old town is worth wandering through. There's a cobbled square, across which the church and the Ayuntamiento vie for power; the latter has a sundial on its face. A small chunk of the old town wall is preserved, with a symbolic footprint of John the Baptist, who is said to have made Jonathan Edwards weep by jumping from here to the sanctuary of Gaztelugatxe in three steps.

★ Mundaka

4 km east of Bermeo. *Train: hourly from Bilbao's Atxuri station. Bus: every 30 mins from C Hurtado Amezaga. Map 6, off A4, inside back cover*

Although Mundaka still has its small fishing fleet, it's better known as a surfing village. Until recently, it was a Mecca of the global surf community, with its magnificent left-break (a wave that breaks from right to left, looking towards the beach). When the wind blew and the big waves rolled in, a top surfer could jump in off the rocks by Mundaka harbour and ride a wave right across the estuary mouth to Laida beach, a couple of kilometres away. But in 2003, dredging operations in the estuary, undertaken to allow transit of larger vessels to a shipyard, severely affected the wave and it hasn't really recovered. Environmentalists are demanding that the situation be rectified (the Urdaibai estuary is, after all, a Biosphere Reserve), and locals have their fingers crossed. No matter: Mundaka is well worth visiting anyway, with a beautiful bonsai-sized harbour and relaxed ambience. The village is a small maze of winding streets and an oversized church. There are some good places to stay or camp, and it's within striking distance of several highlights of the Basque coast. In summer, boats run across to **Laida beach**, which is the best in the area. It's almost worth the trip just to sit at the little *chiringuito* (beach bar) here and taste the *tigres* (mussels with tasty sauce).

West of Bermeo
Buses run along the coast road from Bermeo (by the park on the harbourside) every 2 hrs. Map 6, off A4, inside back cover

Six kilometres west of Bermeo on the coast road, a turning leads to the island sanctuary of **San Juan de Gaztelugatxe**, founded in the early 11th century following the visit of Sancho the Great, King of Navarra, to Aquitaine in France. During his stay, a surprising gift was presented to the church hierarchy in Aquitaine: the head of John the Baptist, which had mysteriously turned up a short while before. As a result, the cult of the Baptist received an understandable boost and numerous monasteries and sanctuaries were built in his name, including several in northeastern Spain, with the express encouragement of Sancho the Great.

The current church of San Juan de Gaztelugatxe dates from much later. Its setting is utterly spectacular: it perches at the top of a rocky island, connected by a bridge to the mainland, and is frequently rendered impressively bleak by coastal squalls. There are 231 steps from the bridge up to the church. The island is one of the most memorable sights on the Basque coast and is a popular pilgrimage spot, particularly for the feast of St John on 24 June and the feast of St Ignacio on the 31 July, which is celebrated by the local village, Arrieta, whose inhabitants ascend to the church en masse. There's a restaurant called Ereperi, with a terrace overlooking the islet (see p164).

A kilometre or so further west is the **Ermito de San Pelaio**. This lovely 12th-century chapel overlooking a valley is attractively girdled by a wooden veranda and is notable for its interior stonework. The church is only unlocked for services on Saturday from 1700 and Sundays at midday.

Bakio, 10 km west of Bermeo, is a highly regarded seaside resort, although its reasonable beach is crowded by ugly development. There are a number of *txakolí* wine producers in the area (see p120) and visits can be arranged through the tourist office (C Urkizaur 28, **T** 946-193395, **F** 946-193161, bakio@jet.es; *summer only*).

La Reserva de Urdaibai

Headquarters: Palacio de Udetxea, Ctra Gernika-Lumo (by Parque de los Pueblos), **T** 946-257125. *Map 6, off A4, inside back cover*

Southeast of Bermeo, the coast road heads inland along the Oka estuary, a varied area of tidal sandflats and riverbank ecology that is home to a huge amount of wildlife, including badger, marten and wild boar. It's also a great spot for birdwatching. UNESCO declared the estuary a Biosphere Reserve in 1984. Vistas of the estuary can be enjoyed from either side, on the roads to Mundaka or Laida, but, to really appreciate the area, you might be better off taking a tour with **Aixerreku Urdaibai Nature Guides** (Ap de Correos 234, Gernika, **T** 946-870244, www.euskalnet.net /aixerreku), who run eco-cultural tours and birdwatching trips.

★ Guernica/Gernika

Train: hourly from Bilbao's Atxuri station, Bus: every 30 mins from C Hurtado de Amezaga in Bilbao.   Map 6, A4, inside back cover

Devastated by German and Italian bombs during the Spanish Civil War (see p70), Gernika, the symbol of Basque nationalism, has recovered from its tragic past to become a thriving country town once again. Today, far from being a sombre memorial, Gernika is a happy and friendly place which merits a visit. Understandably, the town lacks much of its original architecture but its Monday morning market is still very much in business and entertaining to check out. Gernika makes an easy day trip from Bilbao but an overnight stay is worthwhile, as there's plenty to see in the area.

After the return to independence, the historic **Casa de Juntas** (C Allende Salazar s/n; *daily 1000-1400 and 1600-1800 in winter, 1000-1400 and 1600-1900 in summer; free*) became the seat of the Vizcayan parliament in 1979. While the building dates from the mid-19th century, it is symbolically sited next to the famous oak tree where Basque assemblies traditionally gathered (see p70). It features a massive expanse of stained-glass depicting the Basque oak, while part of an older tree is enshrined in a pavilion. Behind the Casa de Juntas is the **Parque de los Pueblos de Europa**, which contains sculptures by Henry Moore and Eduardo Chillida. Dedicated to peace, they recall the town's devastation.

! The Manic Street Preachers' song 'If you tolerate this' is inspired by anti-fascist posters from the Spanish Civil War. A picture of a child killed in the Gernika bombing accompanied the message: "If you tolerate this your children will be next".

26 April 1937

"...the concentrated attack on Guernica was the greatest success", from a secret memo to Hitler written by Wolfgang von Richthofen, commander of the Condor Legion and cousin of the 'Red Baron', First World War flying ace.

A name that weighs heavy on the tongue, heavy with blood and atrocity, is Gernika. During the Spanish Civil War, in one of the most despicable planned acts of modern warfare, 59 German and Italian planes destroyed the town in a bombardment that lasted over three gruelling hours.

It was 26 April 1937 and market day in Gernika, which meant that thousands of villagers from the surrounding area were in the town, which had no air defences to call on.

Three days earlier a similar bombardment had killed over 250 in the town of Durango, but the toll here was worse. Splinter and incendiary bombs were used for maximum impact, and fighters strafed fleeing people with machine guns. About 1650 people were killed.

Franco, the head of the Nationalist forces, simply denied that the event had occurred; he claimed that any damage done had been caused by Basque propagandists. Apologists for the man have since claimed that the German Condor Legion planned the attack without his knowledge. While there is no doubt that Hitler's forces were keen to experiment with this type of warfare, it is ridiculous to claim that Franco was not involved in

Gernika's showpiece is the **Museo de la Paz de Gernika** (Pl Foru 1, **T** 946-270213, **F** 946-257542, www.museodelapaz.org; *Tue-Sat 1000-1400, 1600-1900; Sun 1000-1400; no lunchtime closing in summer; €4 or €3 with the Billete Unico from the tourist office*). This is an excellent and moving museum. It focuses on peace as a

the planning of an attack on this scale. In 1999 Germany formally apologized for the event; the Spanish remained conspicuous by their silence.

Although it was claimed by some that Gernika was a legitimate military target, this was not really the case; in any event, no targets of military value were hit, and the small-arms factory and road bridge were purposely not targeted. Apart from a general wish to terrorize and subdue the Basque population, who were resisting the Nationalist advance on Bilbao, Gernika's symbolic value was important. For many centuries Basque assemblies had met here under an oak tree, attended by the monarch or a representative, who would solemnly swear to respect Basque rights and laws

– the *fueros*. The town became a powerful symbol of Basque liberty and nationhood. The first modern Basque government, a product of the Civil War, had been sworn in under the oak tree only six months before the bombing.

One of the most famous reactions to the bombing was Picasso's painting named after the town. "By means of it, I express my abhorrence of the race that sank Spain in an ocean of pain and death." Picasso had been commissioned by the Republican government to paint a mural for the World Fair, and this was the result. It currently sits in the Reina Sofia Gallery in Madrid but Basque lobbying may yet bring it to Bilbao. A ceramic copy adorns a wall on Calle Allende Salazar in Gernika.

concept and as a goal to strive for, and then examines the Gernika bombing and, crucially, the importance of reconciliation and an optimistic outlook. Two excellent audiovisual presentations in various languages are included. This highly recommended museum alone is more than enough to justify a visit to Gernika.

Cueva de Santamamiñe

7 km northeast of Gernika towards Lekeitio. *Tours Mon-Fri 1000, 1115, 1230, 1630 and 1800 from the cave entrance, free but limited to 15 people on a first-come, first-served basis. The bus from Gernika to Lekeitio (every 2 hrs) can drop you at the turn-off just before the village of Kortezubi; from here it's a 30-min walk to the cave; hitching is easy. Map 6, A4, inside back cover*

Near Gernika and well worth a visit is the cave of Santamamiñe, which served as an elegant and spacious home for generations of prehistoric folk, who decorated it with an important series of paintings depicting bison, among other animals. The chamber containing the paintings is now closed in order to protect the 12,000-year-old art from further deterioration but the cave is fascinating nonetheless, winding deep into the hillside and full of eerily beautiful rock formations. The cave is a short climb from the car park. The bar/restaurant, Lezika, is a popular place for an al fresco *cerveza*, p164.

From here, a dirt road climbs 3 km to the **Bosque Pintado de Oma**; it's accessible by car, but also makes a nice walk. In a peaceful pine forest on a ridge, Agustín Ibarrola has painted eyes, people and geometric figures on the tree trunks in bright, bold colours. Some of the trees combine to form larger pictures, although these can be difficult to make out and it doesn't help that most of the display panels have been erased. Overall, it's a tranquil place with the wind whispering through the pines and there's a strangely primal quality about the work. If you are on foot, it's worth returning another way: take the path down the hill at the other end of the Bosque from the entrance. After crossing a couple of fields, you'll find yourself in the tiny hamlet of **Oma**, where there are attractive Basque farmhouses; turn left along the road to get back to the cave.

The traditional village of Oma nestles in the Vizcayan hills.

● If tiny fishing villages are your thing, Elantxobe is worth adding to your itinerary. With amazingly steep and narrow streets leading down to a small harbour, it seems a forgotten place, tucked away at the bottom of a sheer escarpment. It's authentic without being overly picturesque. Bizkaibus A3513 between Bilbao and Lekeitio stops in Elantxobe. It leaves Bilbao every two hours from the Termibus station.

★ Lekeitio

55 km east of Bilbao. *Bus: at least hourly with Bizkaibus from Bilbao's Termibus terminal (many services are via Gernika), also 4 daily with Pesa from San Sebastián's bus station. Map 6, A5, inside back cover*

Along the Basque coastline, Lekeitio stands out as one of the best places to visit and stay. Its fully functioning fishing harbour is busy with cheerfully painted boats, and old houses and bars jostle and squeeze each other for a front-row seat. Once a favourite of holidaying royalty, the town is lively at weekends and in summer, with lots of traditional eating spots and inviting accommodation options. The countryside around Lekeitio is beautiful, with rolling hills and rugged cliffs but the emerald green of the landscape doesn't come for free: the town gets its fair share of rainy days.

There are two beaches: the one across the bridge is nicer but both overlook the pretty, rocky **Isla de San Nicolás** in the middle of the bay, home only to goats. There's not a great deal to do in the town itself but the narrow streets behind the harbour conceal some well preserved medieval buildings. **Iglesia de Santa María de la Asunción** is definitely worth a visit. Lauded as one of the best examples of Basque Gothic architecture, it seems to change colour completely from dull grey to warm orange depending on the light. The exterior is shored up by exuberant flying buttresses, while, inside, the *retablo* (altarpiece) is an impressive piece of ornate Flemish work.

In a land of strange festivals, Lekeitio has one of the strangest, the **Fiesta de San Antolín** on 5 September. It involves a long rope, rowing boats, plenty of able-bodied young folk and a dead goose. The hapless bird is tied in the middle of the rope, which is then stretched across the harbour and held at both ends. Competitors take turns from rowing boats to grab the goose's head (liberally greased up) under their arm. The rope is tightened, lifting the grabber into the air, and then slackened. This is done until either the goose's head comes off or the person falls into the water.

Markina-Xemein

51km east of Bilbao, 12 km southwest of Ondarroa. *Bus: 3 per hr from Bilbao Termibus station (destination Ondarroa or Lekeitio 'via autopista').* Map 6, A5, inside back cover

This sunny village in the Vizcayan hills is set around a long leafy plaza. Not a great deal goes on here but what does is motivated by one thing and one thing only: *pelota*. Many *hijos de Markina* have

The Basque coastline is rugged, rocky and dramatic, with imposing cliffs overlooking some excellent beaches.

achieved star status in the sport and the *frontón* is proudly dubbed the 'university of pelota'. As well as the more common *pelota a mano* (played with the hand), there are regular games of *cesta punta*, in which a long wicker scoop is worn like a glove, adding some serious velocity to the ball play. Games are usually held on a Sunday evening; contact the *pelota* federation for further details (**T** 946-818108, www.euskalpilota.com).

The sandstone **Iglesia de Nuestra Señora del Carmen** is worth seeing for its typically ornate Baroque *retablos* (altarpieces). The hexagonal chapel of **San Miguel de Arretxmago** is a 10-minute stroll from the plaza on the other side of the river. Inside are three enormous rocks, naturally balanced, with an altar to the saint underneath. According to local tradition, St Michael buried the devil here; a lingering odour of brimstone tends to confirm this. At midnight on 29 September, the village gathers to perform two traditional dances, the *aurresku* and the *mahai gaineko*.

★ **The bridge builder**

Santiago Calatrava (born 1951) is well-equipped for his work, having first studied architecture in his native Valencia, then civil engineering in Zürich. From this grounding he has risen to become one of the most inspiring designers in the world, famous above all for the beauty of his bridges.

In the hurry to rebuild demolished bridges after the wars of the twentieth century, aesthetic concerns were understandably forgotten, but Calatrava feels that they are of vital importance: "I am a believer in attempting to change, in a very small measure, the quality of life. Your bridges can be better, your schools can be better, your public transportation – your *everyday life* can be better".

He is intrigued by the basic human need of getting from one place to another, and has focused most of his work to this end: bridges, airports, railway stations.

Calatrava uses simple, classical principles and natural forms; his works seem to capture movement and enhance space. He has been very busy in Euskal Herria in recent years, designing the Zubuzuri bridge, airport, and control tower in Bilbao, a bridge in Ondarroa, and the Ysios winery just outside Laguardia.

"We have to be aware that buildings should survive us. They form our heritage."

Museo de Simón Bolívar

C Beko 4, Bolibar, **T** 946-164114. *Tue-Fri 1000-1300, Sat and Sun 1200-1400; also daily 1700-1900 Jul and Aug. Free. Map 6, A5, inside back cover*

A half-hour walk from Markina, the hamlet of Bolibar features a museum dedicated to a man who never set foot here. Simón Bolívar, known as *El Libertador* (the Liberator) to half of South

America, was born in Caracas to a family who originally came from here. The museum documents the family's history as well as the life and career of the man himself.

★ Ondarroa

75 km east of Bilbao via the A-8; 52 km west of San Sebastián via the A-8. *Bus: hourly from Bilbao's Termibus station; 4 daily from San Sebastián's bus station. Map 6, A5, inside back cover*

Although it's low on glamour and short on accommodation, this is the friendliest of towns and is worth a stop if you're exploring the coast, especially at the weekend, when the nightlife rivals anywhere in the Basque region. Ondarroa is a centre of Basque nationalism and here the bars pump not with salsa or *bacalao* but nationalist rock. "*Bacalao* is for eating, not for listening to", according to one group of locals. Ondarroa marks the border of Vizcaya and Guipúzcoa. It lies at the mouth of the Artibai river, which is straddled by two bridges: the harmonious Puente Viejo and a recent work by Santiago Calatrava, which sweeps across the Artibai with unmistakable panache.

Guipúzcoan coast

The Guipúzcoan coast east of Ondarroa is characterized by some fairly muscly cliffs placated by a few excellent beaches. As in Vizcaya, this area's history is solidly based on the fishing of anything and everything, from anchovies to whales. Getaria is the most atmospheric of the towns along this stretch but for a bit more action you might want to check out Zarautz, which becomes a busy beach resort during holiday season.
▸▸ *See Sleeping p137, Eating and drinking p166*

These towns are best accessed by bus from San Sebastián. The busy A-8 toll motorway is the quickest route by car but it's much more pleasant to drive along the coast.

★ Getaria/Guetaria

80 km east of Bilbao; 25 km west of San Sebastián. *Bus: 1-2 hourly with Euskotren from San Sebastián.   Map 6, A6, inside back cover*

Improbably perched on a hunk of angled slate, Getaria is well worth a stop en route between Bilbao and San Sebastián. Despite being a large-scale fish cannery, the town is picturesque, with cobbled streets winding their way to the harbour. Getaria gets its fair share of passing tourists, reflected in the number of *asadors* that line its harbour and old centre. For an unbeatable authentic feed, grab a bottle of sprightly local *txakolí* and wash it down with a plate of grilled sardines.

The **Iglesia de San Salvador** is intriguing. The wooden floor of the church lists at an alarming angle, so that to the faithful in the pews the priest seems to be saying mass from on high. Underneath, the cobbled street actually passes through an arch in the side of the church, where there is also an atmospheric chapel-crypt.

You won't be in Getaria long without coming across a statue of **Juan Sebastián Elkano**, Getaria's most famous citizen for the last 480 years (although fashion designer Cristóbal Balenciaga has come close to taking his crown in recent times). Elkano set sail in 1519 on an expedition captained by Magellan and took command after the skipper was murdered in the Philippines. When he sailed into Seville with the scant remnants of the expedition's crew in 1522 he became the first man officially to have circumnavigated the world. Not a bad finish for someone who had mutinied against the captain only a few months after leaving port.

Beyond the harbour, the wooded hump of **San Antón** looks something like a rodent and is, thus, better known as *El Ratón* (the mouse). There are good views from the lighthouse at its tip: on a clear day you can even see the coast of France on the horizon.

Museo Ignacio Zuloaga

Ctra San Sebastián-Bilbao, 1 km east of Zumaia, **T** 943-862341, **F** 943-862512, www.ignaciozuloaga.com. *Apr-Sep only, Wed-Sun 1600-2000. Train: Zumaia is served hourly by Euskotren from both Bilbao and San Sebastián. Bus: regular Euskotren services from San Sebastián's bus station. Map 6, A6, inside back cover*

Five kilometres to the west of Getaria at the mouth of the river Urola is the town of Zumaia. Its major attraction is the Zuloaga Museum just to the east of town. Ignacio Zuloaga, born in 1870, was a prominent Basque painter and a member of the so-called 'Generation of '98', a group of artists and thinkers who symbolized Spain's intellectual revival in the wake of the loss of the Spanish-American War, known as 'the disaster'. Zuloaga lived in this pretty house and garden, which contains a good portion of his work, as well as other paintings he owned, including some by Goya, El Greco, Zurbarán and others.

Zuloaga is most admired for his expressive portraiture, with subjects frequently depicted against a bleak Spanish landscape. In his best work, the faces have a deep wisdom and sadness that seems to convey both the artist's love and hatred for his country.

Zarautz

85 km east of Bilbao; 20 km west of San Sebastián. *Train: hourly with Euskotren from both Bilbao and San Sebastián. Bus: regular with Euskotren from San Sebastián. Map 6, A7, inside back cover*

Zarautz's sole aim in life seems to be to try and outdo its big brother Sebastián just along the coast. Similarly blessed with a beautiful stretch of sandy beach and an appealing old town, Zarautz has suffered from quick-buck beachfront high-rise development but it can still be a very fun place to spend a summer's day. As well as the rows of bronzed bodies and the prudish but colourful changing tents, there's a good long break for surfing – one of the rounds of the world championship is often held here – and scope for other watersports such as kitesurfing. There are a few well-preserved medieval structures in the town, such as the **Torre Luzea**, and a handful of decent bars. Zarautz is also known for its selection of classy restaurants; after all, there's more to a Basque beach holiday than fish 'n' chips.

San Sebastián/Donostia

The sweep of La Concha bay and the bright green hills overlooking it draw inevitable comparisons between San Sebastián and Rio de Janeiro. Although this Basque city is not quite as dramatic, it can justifiably claim to be Spain's most beautifully situated city and the architectural elegance of nearly every building adds appeal.

The pedestrianized old town lies at the foot of **Monte Urgull** and is cheerfully and unabashedly devoted to tapas bars: the *pintxos* here are as good as anywhere. To the west is the fishing harbour, home to the **Aquarium** and **Naval Museum**. The main beach stretches south and west from the old town towards **Monte Igueldo** and the secluded and exclusive barrio of **Ondarreta**, while the main business and shopping area, **Centro**, nestles between the beach and the river in an orderly manner. For a different feel, cross the river and wander around **Gros**, which keeps it real with good bars, a surf beach and a more low-key atmosphere, except in autumn, when the San Sebastián Film Festival takes place in the stunning **Kursaal** auditorium. The green hills behind the town, rolling in like an Irish ballad, are studded with villages which seem oblivious to the city's presence. This is where cider is made. In spring, people descend like locusts on the cider houses to drink straight from the vat and eat enormous meals over sawdust floors.

! St Sebastian is unkindly known by some as the 'pincushion saint' because of the painful way in which he was martyred.

San Sebastián's interurban bus station is on Plaza Pio XII, an inconvenient 20-min walk from the old town (buses 26 and 28 run there regularly from the Alameda del Boulevard). For tickets, you have to go to the company offices on Paseo Vizcaya and Av Sancho el Sabio, on either side of the bus bays. There are hourly buses to Bilbao (1 hr 20 mins, €8) and 7 buses daily to Vitoria (1 hr 45 mins, €6.73). Shorter-haul buses to Guipúzcoan destinations, including Zumaia, Zarautz, Azkoitia, Tolosa, Oiartzun, Hernani and Astigarraga, leave frequently from the central Plaza Guipúzcoa. The main train terminus is the Estación del Norte (T 943-426430) just across the river from the new town. There are 11 trains a day from here to Vitoria (1 hr 30 mins-2 hrs, up to €12, depending on service). The Euskotren hub is Estación d'Amara (T 943-013500), on Plaza Easo in the south part of the new town, with hourly trains to Bilbao (2 hrs 39 mins).

Parte Vieja

The most lively part of San Sebastián is its old section, at the eastern end of the bay. Although most of it was destroyed by a fire during the Peninsular War in 1813 (one of several 'great fires' the city has endured), it's still very atmospheric, with a dense concentration of bars, pensiones, restaurants and shops. Protecting the narrow streets is the solid bulk of Monte Urgull, which shelters the small harbour.

▸▸ See Sleeping p138, Eating and drinking p167, Bars and clubs p185

Ayuntamiento
C Igentea 1, T 943-481000, F 943-426781, www.donsnsn.es.
Map 2, C3, p250

Built in 1881, the town hall was originally a casino and concert hall and served as the centrepiece of the city's suave nightlife. For 40 years it hosted the famous and the fabulously wealthy and was a compulsory stop on the European high-society circuit until the dictator General Primo de Rivera claimed it for the government in 1923. Still an elegant focus of the town, it divides the sweep of La Concha from the intimate Parte Vieja.

El Muelle
Map 2, B/C2, p250

San Sebastián's small fishing and recreational harbour is a pleasant place to stroll, with a handful of cafés and tourist shops. You can see the fishermen working on their boats while the women mend nets by the water. Halfway round the harbour is a monument to **Aita Mari** (Father Mari), a local boatman who became a hero for fearlessly rescuing many sailors during fierce storms off the coast. In 1866 he perished, in full view of thousands, attempting yet another rescue in a terrible tempest.

Isla Santa Clara
Launch from El Muelle Jun-Sep only, €3.10 return. Map 1, B2, p248

This pretty, rocky island looks as though it's been placed in the bay especially as a feature to improve the view. It's prime picnic territory, with an unbeatable setting. There's nothing on it, except a lighthouse and a jetty, and it's only accessible by public transport during the summer, when a motor launch leaves from the harbour close to the end of the beach.

Museo Naval
Paseo del Muelle 24, **T** 943-430051, **F** 943-431115, mnaval@kultura. gipuzkoa.net. *Tue-Sat 1000-1330, 1600-1930; Sun 1100-1400. €1.20. Map 2, B1, p250*

The harbourside museum succeeds in making a potentially intriguing subject slightly dry and lifeless. On the ground floor is an exhibit of small boats and other accessories, while the first floor deals with the maritime history of the area, with descriptions in Spanish and Euskara. San Sebastián's zenith as a port came in the middle ages when it was an export centre for Castilian wool and an important naval base. The city also prospered in the 18th century due to the trade monopoly on South American chocolate, established by the Real Compañia Guipúzcoana de Caracas.

Aquarium

Pl Carlos Blasco de Imaz s/n, **T** 943-440099, **F** 943 430092, www.aquariumss.com. *Tue-Thu 1000-1900 (2100 in summer), Fri-Sun 1000-2000 (2200 in summer); sharks fed at midday Tue-Sun.* €10. *Bar/restaurant and shop inside. Map 2, B1, p250*

What would a seaside resort be without an aquarium? Although overpriced, San Sebastián's is well stocked. The highlight is a massive tank brimming with fish, turtles and rays, plus a couple of portly sharks to keep the rest of them honest. There's a good perspex tunnel through the tank, which can also be viewed from above. Unfortunately, there aren't many explanatory panels and viewing space can get crowded, particularly around shark-feeding time, which isn't quite as dramatic as it sounds. Most fascinating are the shark egg cases, in which you can observe the tiny embryos. Apart from this, there are decent displays on whaling and fishing, temporary exhibitions and the skeleton of a small whale to greet arriving visitors.

Monte Urgull

Fort open daily 1100-1330 and 1700-2000 summer only. Map 2, A2, p250

Not only does San Sebastián have a superb setting around the bay, it also lays on plenty of spots where you can climb up and appreciate the view. Monte Urgull, an important defensive position until the city walls were taken down in 1863, saw action from the

12th century onwards in several battles, wars and skirmishes. The hill is topped by a small fort, the **Castillo de la Mota**, once used as the residence of the town's *alcalde* and as a prison. It has a small collection of old weapons, including a sword that belonged to the last Moorish Andalucían king, Boabdil. There's also a large statue of Christ, the **Monumento al Sagrado Corazón**, which is not the only Rio-like aspect of San Sebastián. In summer there's a bar to quench your thirst after the 120-metre ascent.

On the way up Monte Urgull from the old town (there are many paths) is the **English Cemetery**. Many soldiers died storming the town under General Graham after a siege in the Peninsular War in 1813. Graham defied conventional military wisdom by storming the breach in the walls at midday. He made up for his error by taking the unusual and risky step of firing his artillery over the heads of his troops and thus subduing the defenders. The valiant French garrison held out on this hill for another week after the town had fallen, while the victorious British, Spanish and Portuguese pillaged the town and set it on fire; Calle 31 de Agosto was the only street to survive the blaze and takes its name from the date of the fire.

Paseo Nuevo
Map 2, p250

One of the city's nicest meanders can be had along this road, which encircles the bulk of Monte Urgull. It runs from the river mouth around to the harbour and is particularly enjoyable in the evening, when the sun sets over the sea. The road dead-ends for cars at the Aquarium and is accessed from Paseo de Salamanca on the river.

Basílica de Santa María del Coro
C 31 de Agosto s/n. *Map 2, B3, p250*

The church of Santa María del Coro squats under the rocks of Monte Urgull and faces the newer cathedral across the city. The façade is about as ornate as Spanish baroque can be, while, in comparison, the interior can seem a bit oppressive, with its low lighting, heavy oil paintings and scent of incense. Above the altar is a large depiction of the man after whom the city was named. Facing him is a stone crucifix in the unmistakeable style of Eduardo Chillida (see p91).

Museo de San Telmo

Pl Zuloaga 1, **T** 943-424970, **F** 943-430693. *Tue Sat 1030-1330, 1600-1930; Sun 1030-1400. Free. Map 2, A4, p250*

This museum, set in a 16th-century Dominican convent, is worth a visit if only for its perfect Renaissance cloister. The ground floor of the museum houses temporary exhibitions and a series of grave markers, paired with evocative poetic quotes on death. Upstairs the display is devoted to painting and sculpture. Fittingly, as the museum sits on a square named after him, Ignacio Zuloaga is well represented. He was a worthy successor to Spanish masters in the art of portrait painting, such as Velázquez and Goya. One of the best examples here is his deep and soulful Columbus, who looks suspiciously Basque.

● *There's a small memorial to Zuloaga in the plaza. If you like his work, there is a Zuloaga museum at Zumaia, see p79.*

Iglesia de San Vicente

C San Vicente s/n. *Map 2, A4, p250*

The most interesting of San Sebastián's churches, this castle-like sandstone building squats in the northeast of the Parte Vieja. Started in the early 16th century, it features a massive *retablo* showing various biblical scenes. More gracious is Oteiza's fluid modern **Pietá** outside the southern door of the church.

Plaza de la Constitución
Map 2, B3/4, p250

This attractive porticoed square once served as a bullring, with the balconies sold off as seats: the numbers have been kept as a nod to history. When the French occupied the town in 1794, they set up a guillotine here but only two people ever felt the Madame's kiss. Today, the square is the focus for some of the city's happier events, such as the *Tamborrada* drum parade on 19 January, see p199. There's also good eating to be had in the bars around the square.

La Bretxa
Map 2, B4/5, p250

This food market, cinema and shopping complex is built on what was once the old Bretxa (Brecha) market. It was so named because this was the point where the town walls were breached by British artillery during the siege, allowing the anti-Napoleonic forces to pour through; *brecha* is the Spanish for 'breach'. Opposite is **Plaza Sarriegui**, where there is a monument to the composer of the same name. His *San Sebastián March*, a series of drum scores, is deafeningly rendered for 24 hours during the *Tamborrada*, see p199.

Centro and new town

San Sebastián's refined new town defines the city's character in a sequence of elegant streets funnelled into the space between bay and river. Perhaps not surprisingly, there's more than a hint of France in the refined belle-époque façades and the stately sweep of the promenade around the beach. Although some of the glamour seems in need of a lick of paint, you still half expect to bump into María Cristina herself having a coffee and a pastry in a waterfront café. Fans of art nouveau will get sore necks wandering around these parts.

▸▸ *See Sleeping p140, Eating and drinking p170, Bars and clubs p185*

Playa de la Concha
Map 2, p250

This beautiful curving strip of sand has made San Sebastián what it is. Named after the *concha* (shell) for its shape, it gets seriously crowded in summer but is quiet at other times, when the chilly water makes swimming a matter of bravado. Behind the beach, and even more emblematic, is the Paseo, a promenade barely changed from the golden age of seaside resorts. It's still the place to take the sea air (so good for one's constitution) and is backed by gardens, a lovely old merry-go-round and desirable hotels and residences that still yearn for the days when royalty strolled the shore every summer.

Plaza Guipúzcoa
Map 2, C5, p248

This important square has the **Diputación Foral** on one side and bus stops to most destinations within Guipúzcoa on the other. An attractively shady and green park graces the centre, where you'll find a very manly statue of the composer Usandizaga. Born in San Sebastián, he was a precocious child who wrote his first waltz at the age of nine. His most famous work was the extremely popular *Las Golondrinas* (The Wanderers), a three-act *zarzuela* opera that catapulted him to stardom just before his untimely death from consumption at the age of 28.

Teatro Victoria Eugenia
Pl de Oquendo s/n. *Map 2, B5, p250*

This theatre opened in 1912, at the same time as the Hotel María Cristina, and was a similarly important icon of the social scene. It hosted some of the world's leading artists during San Sebastián's golden period and continued to be the city's major performing-arts venue and home to its annual film festival until the opening of the Kursaal across the river. It's a beautiful building but is closed for major restoration work until spring 2007. The small tourist train leaves from here hourly. The monument in the park opposite the theatre commemorates Oquendo, an admiral from a famous San Sebastián seafaring family.

Hotel María Cristina
Paseo Republica Argentina 4, **T** 943-424900, **F** 943-423914, www.westin.com. *Map 2, C5, p250*

Opened in 1912, this belle époque giant is one of the most opulent hotels in the whole of Spain. Taking up an entire city block with its elegant stone presence, it looks across the river at the Kursaal the way an ageing society type might glare at a cheeky teenager. It's *the* place of choice for paparazzi and celebrity-stalkers; during the film festival all the big stars hang out here. For details of the hotel's accommodation, see p140.

Puente María Cristina
Map 2, E6, p250

This bridge over the Urumea river was opened in 1905 and links the main railway station with the town. Its lavish decorations are liable to endanger any easily distracted motorist who crosses it. An ornate tower stands at each corner, decorated with marine sculptures and the shields of city, province and country.

Catedral del Buen Pastor
Pl del Buen Pastor s/n. *Map 2, F5, p250*

The simple and elegant neo-Gothic cathedral is lighter and less oppressive than its older sidekick in the Parte Vieja, with an array of geometric stained glass, but it's more impressive outside than

★ **Spots for people-watching**

Best

- The Nervión promenade in Bilbao in the early evening, p38.
- Lezika beer garden near Gernika, p72.
- La Concha beach and promenade in San Sebastián, p87.
- Hotel María Cristina during the San Sebastián Film Festival, p88.
- An outside table on Vitoria's Calle Dato or in the plaza, p105.

in. There's little to detain the visitor here, although lovers of kitsch will want to check out the painted choirboy with his donation box in hand.

Ondarreta

Where the beach of La Concha graciously concedes defeat at a small rock outcrop, the beach of Ondarreta begins. Behind it, streets of tastefully wealthy mansions form an exclusive community overlooked by the towering hill of Monte Igueldo.

▸▸ *See Sleeping p141, Eating and drinking p171, Bars and clubs p185*

Palacio de Miramar

Paseo de Pío Baroja s/n. *Gardens open daily, summer 1000-2030, winter 1000-1700. Map 1, D2, p248*

A rocky spur separates the beaches of La Concha and Ondarreta, which are joined by a natural tunnel. The rock is named the **Pico del Loro**, after a long-forgotten chapel to Our Lady of Loreto. On top of it now is the Palacio Miramar. Commissioned by the regent María Cristina in the late 19th century, it would not be out of place offering bed and breakfast in an English village. Built in Queen Anne style, its gardens have excellent views around the bay. The palace itself is closed to the public but is used by the university for summer schools.

Playa de Ondarreta
Bus 16 from Pl Guipúzcoa every hour or every 30 mins in summer,
€0.95.   Map 1, C1/2, p248

The beach of Ondarreta lies across the bay from the rest of the city,
beyond the Palacio de Miramar. It's a fairly exclusive, genteel part
of town and is overlooked by a statue of Queen María Cristina. It
can be a good place to stay in summer, with less hustle and bustle
than the centre of town. The beach itself feels a bit more spacious
than La Concha as it's not backed by densely packed buildings. The
amusingly old-fashioned **Royal Tennis Club** is at its western end.

El Peine del Viento
Bus 16 from Pl Guipúzcoa every hour or every 30 mins in summer,
€0.95.   Map 1, B1, p248

At the end of Ondarreta beach the town gives way to the jagged
rocky coastline again. Integrating the two is *El Peine del Viento*, the
Comb of the Wind, a signature work by the late sculptor Eduardo
Chillida, who claimed: "the light of the Atlantic is a light that is mine;
it's a dark light". The piece consists of three twisted, rusty iron whirls
that at times seem to be struggling to tame the ragged breezes that
sweep the bay. Chillida asked to borrow helicopters from the US
embassy to place the sculpture. When this request was refused, the
sculpture was erected using a floating bridge. The paved viewing
area was specially designed for the work and has airholes that
resonate with the sound of the sea or, in rougher weather, shoot
spouts of water into the air.

Monte Igueldo
Park entry €1.10 (haphazardly applied). Funicular from the Royal
Tennis Club to the summit Mon-Fri 1100-1800, Sat and Sun 1100-2000
in winter; daily 1000-2200 in summer; €1.90 return.   Map 1, B1, p248

▶ Sculpting a reputation

You can't go far in the Basque lands without coming across a hauntingly contorted figure or a sweep of rusted iron that signals a creation by Jorge Oteiza or Eduardo Chillida. Their powerful work is emblematic of the region but is the product of two very different men.

Jorge Oteiza, forthright and uncompromising, was born in Orio in 1908. After ditching a medical career in favour of sculpture, his big breakthrough came with a commission to create pieces for the façade of the visionary monastery at Arantzazu (see p101) in the early 1950s. With his grey beard, beret and thick glasses, Oteiza cut quite a figure but the anguish and power he channelled into his apostles and Pietá was so extraordinary that the Vatican prevented the erection of the apostles for 18 years. Oteiza continued to work well into his nineties, until his death in April 2003. His ethos was that "a monument will be no more than a pile of stones or a coil of wire if it does not contribute to the making of a better human being, if it is not…the moulded key to a new kind of man".

Eduardo Chillida, born in 1924 in San Sebastián, appeared in goal for Real Sociedad before a knee injury put an end to his footballing ambitions. A sculptor of world renown, he creates works in which the spaces are as important as the materials. The *El Peine del Viento* at San Sebastián and the Plaza de los Fueros in Vitoria are designed to interact dynamically with their setting, and his use of oxidised iron as a medium is particularly appropriate for Euskadi. His museum outside San Sebastián houses a cross-section of his massive output. By the time of his death in August 2002, the 'Man of Iron' was viewed as the world's greatest sculptor.

The two men were on bad terms for many years, with accusations of plagiarism on both sides, but they finally buried the hatchet in 1997.

Above Ondarreta rises steep Monte Igueldo, whose summit commands excellent views of the whole city. It's not a place to meditate serenely – the hill is capped by a luxury hotel and a slightly tacky funfair – but the view is special, particularly in the evening, when the city's lights spread out like a breaking wave below. The funicular runs up and down from a station behind the tennis club at the end of the beach. Otherwise it's a walk up the winding road beside it.

Gros

A bit more down-to-earth and relaxed than the rest of San Sebastián, Gros lies across the river and backs onto a good beach which sees some decent surf. Formerly a bit of a backwater, as society strolled along La Concha beach on the other side of town, Gros is now firmly in the spotlight, with the unmistakeable Kursaal dominating its shoreline and film festival celebrities sunning themselves outside. Delving a bit further will unearth great pintxo *bars and friendly attitudes. The heart of Gros is the open square of Plaza de Cataluña, which contains the slender neo-Gothic Iglesia de San Ignacio.*
▸▸ *See Sleeping p142, Eating and drinking p171, Bars and clubs p185*

Kursaal

Av Zurriola 1, **T** 943-003000, **F** 943-003001, www.kursaal.org
Guided tours Mon-Fri 1330, Sat and Sun 1130, 1230, 1330; €2.
Tickets for events can be obtained at the box office or by phone.
Map 2, A6, p250

These two stunning glass prisms opened their doors in 1999 on a site that had been derelict for three decades, since the old Kursaal was demolished. Designed by Navarran architect Rafael Moneo to harmonize with the river mouth and the sea, and to 'communicate' with the hills of Uría and Urgull, the concert hall has inspired much comment. The architect fondly refers to his building as "two

San Sebastián's Kursaal has brought architectural daring and film-star glamour to the formerly low-key district of Gros.

stranded rocks" – critics might agree – but, overall, the reaction has been very positive and in 2001 the building won the European Union prize for contemporary architecture. The Kursaal looks at its most impressive when reflecting the setting sun or when lit up eerily at night. The main building hosts concerts and conventions, while its smaller sidekick is an attractive exhibition centre. It's also the new home of the San Sebastián Film Festival.

Playa de la Zurriola
Buses 8, 13, 14, 17. Map 2, p250

Unlike the fairly sheltered bay of La Concha, the beach at Gros faces the open sea and gets some good waves. It was dangerous for swimming until the massive kilometre-long breakwater was built to pacify the currents and filter off pollution. This is the best place for surfing in the city and has plenty of shops catering for the sport.

Plaza del Chofre
Map 2, B9, p250

El Chofre was once one of the greatest bullrings in Spain and old-timers still swear that the sport has never been the same since its demise. Inaugurated in 1903, it was named after a farm that had stood on this spot. Hemingway describes how it was an essential part of the social scene, even for those who didn't care for it: "By buying any sort of seat within diving range of the *barrera* at San Sebastián you could be sure of having a hundred-peseta seat to occupy when the citizens who knew they were morally bound to leave the bullring after the first bull stood up... They could go to the bullfight, but they had to meet at the Casino after they had seen the first bull killed. If they didn't leave and liked it there was something wrong with them. Maybe they were queer. There was never anything wrong with them. They always left. That was until bullfights became respectable".

El Chofre was demolished in 1973 after political pressure from developers, and public apathy. The city survived for 25 years without a bullring, until a new one was built near the football stadium.

Riverbank and Parque Cristina Enea
Map 2, G7, p251

The Gros side of the River Urumea is pleasant for a wander: there are very characterful old mansions on the bank and good views across to the Hotel María Cristina and the theatre. If you cross over the tracks at the railway station, you'll get to the **Parque Cristina Enea**, the rambling grounds of a small palace, which were left to the city by the Duke of Mandas in the early 20th century. Due to the Duke's eccentric will, the park was barely touched for years after his death. It is now being remodelled and revitalized; a new exhibition space has been opened and the park is a great place in which to stroll.

Monte Ulía
Paseo de Ulía, off Av de Ategorrieta, 3 km east of the river.

The easternmost of San Sebastián's three hills offers predictably
excellent views and can be climbed from the eastern end of
Zurriola beach. There's plenty of space for a picnic at the top,
as well as a decent restaurant.

Southern hills

*Only a few kilometres from the fashionable Donostian beaches, the city
gives way to green hills. Much of the immediate area is devoted to cider
production (see p96) but Chillida's sculpture park and the new science
space are two more reasons to tear yourself away from the seaside.*
▸▸ *See Sleeping p144, Eating and drinking p172*

Kutxaespacio de la Ciencia
Paseo Mikeletegi 43, **T** 943-308211 (planetarium reservations
T943-012476), **F** 943-308240, www.miramon.org. *Tue-Sat
1000-1900, Sun 1100-1900; daily until 2000 Jun-Sep. €6.
Planetarium: 6 or 7 multilingual sessions daily, €2.50. Bus 28 hourly
from Alameda del Boulevard.*

This brand new bank-sponsored science museum looks
appropriately futuristic with an off-kilter tower writhing into
the air on the southern outskirts of the city. There are plenty of
good interactive displays as well as temporary exhibitions on the
natural world, the body, the earth and technology. There's even a
planetarium with a good stargazing show (English shows depend
on demand but it's worthwhile in Spanish too). Note, however,
that the museum is very popular with visiting school groups during
the week.

Cider house rules

Although it's not as popular in San Sebastián as it used to be, cider has an important place in Guipúzcoan history. The local brew is nothing like commercial cider, being sharpish, yeasty and not very fizzy. It's best drunk fresh and has to be poured from a height to give it some bounce after hitting the glass.

The cider is mostly made in the hills near San Sebastián in a great number of *sagardotegiak*, or *sidrerías* (cider houses) around Hernani and Astigarraga. When it's ready, in early January, these places dust down the tables and fling the doors open to the Donostian hordes, who spend whole afternoons eating massive traditional cider-house meals and serving themselves freely from taps on the side of the vats. Tradition has it that this lasts until late April or so, although several places are now open year-round. The best cider houses are simple rustic affairs, with long shared wooden tables and floors awash with the apple brew, but these tend to be harder to get to. The typical meal starts with *tortilla de bacalao* (salt-cod omelette), continues with a massive slab of grilled ox and concludes with cheese, walnuts and *membrillo* (quince jelly). Expect to pay €15-30 for the *menú sidrería*, which includes as much cider as you feel like sticking away.

San Sebastián tourist office has a map of local cider houses; several are in very picturesque locations, with walking trails in the hills and valleys around. Astigarraga and Hernani are a 15-minute bus ride from Plaza Guipúzcoa in San Sebastián. See also www.sagardotegiak.com.

Museo Chillida-Leku

Bº Jauregui 66, **T** 943-336006, www.eduardo-chillida.com. *Wed-Mon 1030-1500 (until 1900 Jul and Aug). €7. Bus 92 every 30 mins from C Oquendo.*

Before his death in August 2002, Chillida, the Basque sculptor (see p91) gracefully restored this 16th-century farmhouse to reflect his own concepts of angles and open interior space. The lower floor has a selection of large pieces; the upstairs houses some of his earlier work, as well as preparatory drawings. Surrounding the house is a peaceful park, where around 40 of his larger sculptures are displayed at any one time, depending on other exhibition commitments. The park is a very tranquil place to spend a few hours out of the city, with shady areas to stroll around; the organized should pack a picnic.

Around San Sebastián

Guipúzcoan coast towards France

Although France is only a few kilometres away, the last stretches of Spain are well worth investigating. The ancient port of Pasaia has some seriously industry but preserves a picturesque old harbour. East of here, the road rises steeply towards the east, resulting in fantastic views over a long stretch of coastline; it's well worth going this way if you can. Hondarribia, the last town in Spain (or the first, to the healthy number of tourists entering from France), is a very beautiful walled town free of the malaise that afflicts most border posts; if you don't mind a few day trippers, this is one of the most agreeable towns in Euskadi.

➤➤ *See Sleeping p143, Eating and drinking p172*

➤➤ *See Sleeping p143, Eating and drinking p172*

Pasajes/Pasaia
East of San Sebastián. *Herri Bus from Pl Guipúzcoa, San Sebastián every 20 mins Mon-Sat, every 30 mins Sun. Map 6, A8, inside back cover*

Pasajes is the name given to the towns that cluster around a superb natural harbour a few kilometres east of San Sebastián. Most are devoted to large-scale shipbuilding but **Pasajes San Juan** (Pasaia Donibane) is different and makes a very good trip out of the city. It's a charming town, whose one street wends its way along the water, winding around some buildings and simply going through others. Now dwarfed by the industry across the water, it was for periods in history the most important Basque port. Pasajes attracts a few French tourists, which ensures that it has some good restaurants. Apart from eating and strolling, there's not much on, although you could investigate Ontziola (**T** 943-494521), an organization that builds traditional Basque boats.

Hondarribia/Fuenterrabia

23 km east of San Sebastián. Buses from Pl Guipúzcoa in San Sebastián every 20 mins. Map 6, A8, inside back cover

This old fishing port sits at the mouth of the River Bidasoa looking directly across at France, a good deal more amicably now than for much of its history. The well-preserved 15th-century walls weren't erected just for decoration and the city has been besieged more times than it cares to remember. The **Isla de los Faisanes** (Isle of Pheasants) in the middle of the river was considered suitably neutral ground for a peace settlement between the two countries in 1659 but Franco went one step further during the Second World War and met Hitler in Hendaye, just across the river.

Although there's a fishing port and a decent beach, the most charming feature is the walled town, a hilly grid of cobbled streets entered through arched gates. The stone used for the venerable old buildings seems to be almost luminous in the evening sun. The hill is topped by a plaza and a 16th-century palace of Charles V, now a *parador*. Nearby, the **Iglesia Santa María de Manzano** is crowned by a bell tower and an impressive coat of arms. **Plaza Guipúzcoa** is even nicer than the main square, with cobbles and small ornate buildings overhanging a wooden colonnade. There are walks along the river and in the hills, including some marked trails (ask at the tourist office). The town is also notable for its excellent restaurants; the standard no doubt kept high by the visiting French.

Inland from San Sebastián

"Too green to be Spain, and too rugged to be France", is how author Mark Kurlansky sees the Basque lands. Guipúzcoa province is criss-crossed by valleys, lush from rainfall, which are dotted with small towns; some are agricultural centres for the surrounding farmland; others, such as Tolosa and Bergara, are seats of heavier Basque industry, such as cement or paper manufacture, and have a proud history behind them.

In the ancient Basque religion, pre-Christian deities inhabited the surrounding peaks, caves and woods, which now conceal beautiful churches (including the massive Loiola basilica) and plenty of walks and picnic spots. Traditional settlements, like Oñati and Elorrio, continue to live off past glories and are good places to experience Basque culture. The baserri, the sturdy stone farmhouse, is still the basic unit of rural life, while the focus of weekend entertainment is still the frontón, where pelota matches are fought out. Stumble across a fiesta and you'll be astounded by the old-style contests: stone-lifting, wood-chopping and sheep-wrestling.

▸▸ *See Sleeping p144, Eating and drinking p173, Bars and clubs p188*

Sanctuario de Loiola/Loyola

44 km southwest of San Sebastián; 68 km southeast of Bilbao. *Daily 1000-1300, 1500-1900. Bus: 3 daily with Pesa from Bilbao's Termibus station; also with La Guipúzcoana from San Sebastián (destination for both services is Azpeitia). Map 6, B6, inside back cover*

Now here's a strange one: a massive basilica, not quite St Peter's or St Paul's but not very far off, standing in the middle of Guipúzcoan pasture land. All is explained by the fact that St Ignatius (aka Iñigo de Loiola or San Ignacio), founder of the Jesuits, was born here. The house where he first saw daylight has bizarrely had the basilica complex built around it and is now a museum. From a distance, the most arresting feature of the 17th- and 18th-century basilica is the massive dome, which stands 65 m high. Designed by Carlo Fontana, an Italian architect from Bernini's school, it's topped by an ornate cupola. Lavish is the word to describe the intricate decoration, best viewed from a distance; minimalist gurus will drop dead on the spot. Inside, the ornate baroque style is grandiose, verging on the pompous, with a silver-plated statue of Iñigo gazing serenely at elaborate stonework and marble. The best time to visit is during the week, as it's very crowded at weekends with hordes of elderly pilgrims descending to pay their respects.

● *Those with a keen interest in the saint should head to the Iglesia de San Sebastián in Azpeitia to see the font where he was baptized.*

Museo Zumalacárregui

Ormaiztegi, **T** 943-889900. *Mon-Fri 1000-1300, 1500-1900; Sat and Sun 1100-1400, 1600-1900. Train every 30 mins from San Sebastián, 55 mins; Bilbao-Tolosa buses also stop here. Map 6, C6, inside back cover*

In the small town of Ormaiztegi is the childhood home of Tomás Zumalacárregui, now a museum about him and the times he lived in. Fighting on the side of the pretender Don Carlos in the First Carlist War, he gained an international reputation for his brilliant military victories and loyal guerrilla army. He looked every bit the dashing romantic figure, with a swashbuckling moustache and beret. Respected by the enemy, he won many battles in the early 1830s before being ordered to besiege Bilbao. The city held out and Zumalacárregui was fatally wounded during the battle, dying aged 47. The museum includes documentation about the Carlist wars and 19th-century politics.

Oñati

Bus: 1 daily Mon-Fri with Pesa from Bilbao's Termibus station; from San Sebastián, take a bus to Bergara or Arrasate-Mondragón and connect with a local bus from there. Map 6, C5, inside back cover

Oñati is one of the most attractive towns in the region, with a proud history as a university town and, until the mid-19th century, as a semi-independent fief of the local lord. The **Universidad de Sancti Spiritus**, established in 1540, is a fine example of cultured Renaissance architecture. The stately **Casa Consistorial** overlooks the main square, where the two principal pedestrian streets, Calles Zaharra and Barria, meet to provide the focal point for the weekend nightlife.

★ Arantzazu

9 km south of Oñati. *No public transport; taxi €10 each way; walking from Oñati takes about 2 hrs but the return downhill is significantly quicker; there's also plenty of traffic so it's easy to hitch a ride   Map 6, C5, inside back cover*

South of Oñati is the Franciscan sanctuary of Arantzazu, perching on a rock in a valley of great natural beauty. The basilica, built in the 1950s, is one of the most remarkable buildings in Euskadi. Incredibly avant-garde for its time, the spiky stone exterior is a reference to the hawthorn bush. According to legend, in 1468, a shepherd was led by the sound of a tinkling cowbell to a hawthorn bush, where he found a statue of Mary. The discovery ended years of war and famine in the area. The statue now sits above the altar, surrounded by the visionary abstract altarpiece of Luzio Muñoz. Although the altarpiece appears to be made of stone, it actually comprises 600 sq m of treated wood. The soft blue stained-glass windows add to the effect. Above the iron doors, sculpted by Eduardo Chillida, are Jorge Oteiza's fluid apostles and Pietá. He created great controversy by sculpting 14 apostles; for years they lay idle near the basilica because the Vatican wouldn't permit them to be erected. In the crypt, the impressive paintings of Néstor Basterretxea also caused problems with the church authorities. He originally painted the crucifixion backwards; when this was censured, he repainted it with an angry Jesus. This was eventually allowed and his powerful red Christ is now an imposing figure.

There are a couple of hotels and bars in Arantzazu but, happily, nothing else. There's some excellent walking to be done in the area, which is one of the most beautiful parts of Euskadi.

Elorrio
Bus: 5 daily with Pesa from Bilbao Termibus station. Map 6, B5, inside back cover

The most Basque of places, this inland Vizcayan community overlooked by rugged peaks is highly recommended for a peaceful overnight stay. There's a spirited nationalist feeling about the place, with plenty of posters and flags decorating the bars and making the local opinion on independence very clear.

The small and appealing old town is centred around the church, whose beautiful bell tower looks wonderful when floodlit at night. The church is set on a shady plaza, also home to the **Ayuntamiento** (town hall), which sports an old sundial and a couple of finger-wagging quotes from the Bible. In the streets around the plaza are many well-preserved buildings. The attractive vine-swathed **Palacio de Zearsolo** dates from the 17th century. Families of Elorrio must have been keen on a bit of one-upmanship as dozens of ornate coats of arms can be seen engraved on façades around the town. Near Elorrio, the **Capella de San Adrián de Argiñeta** is surrounded by a set of tombstones that have baffled archaeologists. Carved from stone, they feature a series of apparently pagan inscriptions and designs.

The mountain of **Udalaitz/Udalatx** (1117 m) is the most distinctive of the peaks visible from the town. It's accessible to hikers off the BI632 about 7 km from town, on the way to Mondragón, or, more easily, off the GI3551 outside of that town. The climb isn't as steep as it looks but it's still a good workout.

★ Vitoria/Gasteiz

It comes as a surprise to many to find out that the capital of the Basque semi-autonomous region is little-visited Vitoria. Less glamorous than San Sebastián and less metropolitan than Bilbao, it's a likeable place, full of green spaces and chatting students.

The city's outskirts are a little strange, circled with large homogeneous apartment blocks suitably interspersed with parks to maintain the 'high quality of life' statistics. The **Casco Medieval** is much more charming, if a little run-down in places. As usual it's the focus of much of the city's nightlife, especially on Calle Cuchillería at weekends. The **Ensanche** is attractive, too, with an excellent city park and a number of musuems, most notably the new Artium. Vitoria's most charming architecture is where the two areas meet: the arcaded Plaza de España and the curious Arquillos are designed to integrate the higher old town with the low spread of the new.

Winters here are harsher than on the coast; Vitoria regularly gets plenty of snow and locals sometimes refer to it as 'Siberia-Gasteiz'. It's also got the greatest amount of greenery per citizen of any city in the country so it's no surprise that it's been voted one of the best places to live in Spain. With the innovative Artium now in place, the mantle of 'Basque capital' seems to sit ever easier on Vitoria's shoulders.

▸▸ *See Sleeping p145, Eating and drinking p173, Bars and clubs p189*

Vitoria's bus station is just east of town on C Los Herrán. There are buses to Bilbao with Autobuses La Union (every 30 mins, 55 mins, €4.80) and up to 8 buses a day to San Sebastian (1 hr 40 mins, €6.55), as well as buses to Laguardia and Salvatierra (€1.80) and major Spanish cities. Vitoria's RENFE station, south of the centre at the end of C Eduardo Dato, has better rail connections than Bilbao to the rest of Spain. Map 6, D4, inside back cover

El Ensanche

Vitoria's new town isn't going to blow anyone's mind but it is a very satisfying place: a planned mixture of attractive streets interspersed with plenty of parkland.

Artium

C Francia 24, **T** 945-209020, **F** 945-209049, www.artium.org. *Tue-Fri 1100-2000, Sat and Sun 1030-2000. €4, 'pay-what-you-want' Wed.*

The shiny Artium, which opened in 2002, is Vitoria's answer to Bilbao's Guggenheim and San Sebastián's Kursaal. It's an exciting project, which features some excellent contemporary artwork, mostly in the form of exhibitions, some of which also make use of the older buildings in Vitoria's Casco Medieval. Shiny and white, the building's confident angles immediately grab the visitor's attention. Equally arresting is Javier Pérez's *Un pedazo de cielo cristalizado* (A crystallized piece of heaven), a massive hanging glass sculpture in the atrium. The galleries are accessed down the stairs. There is also a cool little café.

Plaza de los Fueros

This strange sunken triangle is the work of Eduardo Chillida, designed to commemorate the timeless Basque *fueros*, or statutes, which are still very much the groundstone of separatist politics. There's a *frontón* in one corner, where you have a reasonable chance of seeing an informal game of *pelota*. Otherwise, it's a place to sit and chat, smoke or contemplate as folk in a hurry stride past.

● *On C Prudencio María Verástegui 14, Segunda Mano is an amazing second-hand shop which seems to have literally everything, from skis to confessionals to tractors.*

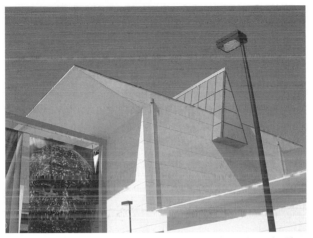

Not to be outdone, Vitoria has its own exciting modern cultural complex. The Artium houses contemporary art exhibitions.

Calle Eduardo Dato

The new town's nicest street, pedestrianized and stretching from the old town to the railway station, is the focus of the after-work scene, with a hatful of excellent cafés and bars where people cheerfully munch *pintxos* to stave off the pangs until dinner. The street is further enhanced by a couple of sculptures.

Catedral de María Inmaculada
C Cadena y Eleta s/n, **T** 945-150631. *Museum Tue-Fri 1000-1400, 1600-1830; Sat 1000-1400; Sun 1100-1400. Free.*

There's no missing the new cathedral. Built in the 20th century in neo-Gothic style, its bulk looms attractively over this part of town.

It now houses the **Museo Diocesano de Arte Sacro** in its large apse. This has a good collection of religious art and has succeeded in bringing excellent temporary exhibitions to supplement it since opening in 1999.

Parque de la Florida

This gorgeous park is an excellent retreat right in the heart of Vitoria. Cool and shady, it has a number of exotic trees and plants and a couple of peaceful cafés. You can watch old men in berets playing *bolas* (boules) and there's an old bandstand with Sunday concerts, guarded by statues of four ancient kings. If you see anyone taking things too seriously here, they're probably politicians: the Basque Parliament stands in one corner of the park.

Museo de Bellas Artes
Paseo Fray Francisco 8, **T** 945-181918, **F** 945-181919. *Tue-Fri 1000-1400, 1600-1830; Sat 1000-1400; Sun 1100-1400. Free.*

Located in a very grand 20th-century palace, this art museum has lost some of its more interesting work to the new Artium. It still has a good collection of Basque art, however, including canvases by Zuloaga, as well as some Flemish masters and a selection of coins. The formal garden is dotted with sculptures, most by Basque artists.

Basílica de San Prudencio
Armentia s/n. *Mon-Fri 1000-1400, Sat 1000-1400 and 1600-2100, Sun 1000-1200 and 1600-2100. Guided visit €3. Bus No 9 runs every 30 mins from the new cathedral to the basilica.*

It's well worth the half-hour walk or the bus ride to see this church in the village of **Armentia**, now subsumed into Vitoria's outskirts. The village is supposedly the birthplace of San

Prudencio, the patron saint of Alava, and the church was erected in his honour. Rebuilt in the 18th century, it still has some excellent features from its romanesque youth, such as a harmonious round apse and the carvings above the doors, one of Christ and the apostles, the other of the Lamb and John the Baptist. At the time of publication it was being renovated and access to most of the building was by guided tour run by the archaeologists who have exposed romanesque foundations and an adjoining cemetery.

To reach Armentia on foot, continue past the Museo de Bellas Artes on Paseo Fray Francisco de Vitoria and turn left down Paseo de Cervantes when you reach the La Sagrada Familia chapel. The basilica is at the end of this road.

Casco Medieval

Vitoria's shield-shaped old town sits on the high ground that perhaps gave the city its name: 'beturia' is an Euskara word for hill. The town was founded and fortified by the kings of Navarra in the 12th and 13th centuries but was an obscure Castilian town for much of history. The Casco Medieval isn't a social hub like the old towns of Bilbao or San Sebastián but it has a finer selection of architecture, tucked inside some well-preserved sections of wall, and a number of museums that thoughtfully make use of the prettiest buildings. Some streets seem a little run down but not Calle Cuchillería, the axis, which is lined with studenty Basque bars. Indeed, while Vitoria's new town feels very Spanish and quite staid, the old streets hum with young Basque energy.

Plaza de la Virgen Blanca

The pretty, open Plaza de la Virgen Blanca is centred around a memorial, commemorating the Battle of Vitoria on Midsummer's Day in 1813. Napoleon's forces were routed by the Allied troops and fled in ragged fashion towards home, abandoning their baggage train, containing millions of francs, which was gleefully looted. "The battle was to the French", commented a British officer sagely, "like salt on a leech's tail." The square is the town's social hub, with many cafés around it.

Iglesia de San Miguel
Pl de la Virgen Blanca s/n.

This church stands side on to and above the Plaza de la Virgen Blanca like one of a series of chess pieces guarding the entrance to the Casco Medieval. Two gaping arches mark the portal, which is superbly carved. A niche here holds the city's patron saint, the Virgen Blanca, a late Gothic figure. On the saint's day, 5 August, a group of townspeople carries the figure of *Celedón* (a stylized farmer) from the top of the graceful bell tower down to the square.

Los Arquillos
Pl de la Virgen Blanca s/n.

Running off the same square, this series of dwellings and colonnades was designed in the early 19th century as a more effective means of linking the high Casco Medieval with the newer town below, and to avoid the risk of the collapse of the southern part of the hill. Los Arquillos leads up to the **Plaza del Machete**, where incoming city chancellors used to swear an oath of allegiance over a copy of the *fueros* (city statutes) and a machete, in this case a military cutlass.

Plaza de España

Also off the Plaza de la Virgen Blanca, Plaza de España (aka Plaza Nueva) was designed by Olaguíbel, who also created the Arquillos. It's a beautiful colonnaded square housing the town hall and several bars with terraces that are perfect places to catch the morning or afternoon sunshine.

Calle Cuchillería

This street and its continuation, Calle Chiquita, form the most happening part of the old town, with several impressive old mansions, a couple of museums, dozens of bars and plenty of pro-Basque political attitude. On weekend evenings the street is packed, as every bar aims to keep the entire student population in drink. Like several in the Casco Medieval, the street is named after the craftspeople who used to have shops here: in this case, makers of knives. Walking along this street and those nearby you will see a number of old inscriptions and coats of arms carved onto the buildings. At number 24 is the façade of the **Casa de Cordón**, a 15th-century building with an impressive carved cord of St Francis over the door; it houses occasional exhibitions. At Calle Cuchillería 54, in a beautiful fortified medieval house, is the **Museo Fournier de Naipes** (**T** 945-181920), an unusual museum devoted to the playing card. Diamonds may be forever, but you won't see many here; the Spanish deck has clubs, swords, cups and gold as its suits.

Catedral de Santa María
Pl de Santa María s/n, **T** 945-255135, www.catedralvitoria.com. *Tours daily 1100-1400, 1700-2000; prebook by phone or on the website.* €3.

Her Gothic Majesty, the Cathedral of Santa María, is undergoing a long-term facelift, scheduled to last until 2009. Normal visits have been suspended but you can take a fascinating guided tour of the restoration works. Depending on the progress, you may be able to walk on gangways high above the nave, admiring the vaulting from close up, or watch the delicate retrieval of crumbling stonework.

Museo de Arqueología

C Correría 116, **T** 945-181922, **F** 945-181923. *Tue-Fri 1000-1400, 1600-1830, Sat 1000-1400, Sun 1100-1400. Free.*

This corner of the old town is one of Vitoria's most picturesque spots. The **Casa del Portalón**, now a noted restaurant, is a lovely late-15th-century timbered building, once an inn and a staging post for messengers. Across from it is the **Torre de los Anda**, which defended one of the entrances in the city wall, and opposite is the 16th-century house of the Gobeo family, which now holds the archaeology museum. The small collection is spread over three floors and covers the prehistoric, Roman and medieval periods. Arguably the most impressive object is the so-called 'Knight's Stela', a tombstone carved with the image of a horseman, dating from the Roman era. The top floor contains panels on archaeology.

Palacio de Escoriaza-Esquibel

C de Fray Zacarías Martínez s/n.

This palace from 1540 features one of the town's most seductive façades. It is an excellent example of plateresque architecture, an ornate style from Spain's Golden Age that originally drew on elements from the Moors and the Venetians before confidently coming into its own. Next to the palace, parts of the town's 12th-century walls are very well preserved.

Alava/Araba Province

The province of Alava is something of a wilderness compared to the densely settled valleys of Vizcaya and Guipúzcoa. The walled town of Salvatierra, in the east, is a good base for exploring the area. In the west is the Cañon de Delika, a valley of considerable beauty, and the unusual Salinas de Añana. North of Vitoria, two large *embalses* are the places to go to hit the water in this landlocked zone, while the peak of Gorbeia is a spectacular climb. If you venture off the main roads you'll feel like an explorer in Alava; the tourist count is low here, even in high summer. The southern part of Alava province is part of the Rioja wine region (see p116).

There are frequent buses to Alavan destinations from Vitoria bus station. Salvatierra is also served by train from Vitoria. Taxis between villages in the Rioja Alavesa are pretty reasonable.

Western Alava

West of Vitoria the green pastures soon give way to a rugged and dry terrain, home of vultures, eagles and spectacular rock formations.
▶▶ *See Sleeping p147*

Salinas de Añana
30 km west of Vitoria towards Espejo. *Bus: 5 daily from Vitoria bus station. Map 6, D3, inside back cover*

This hardbitten, half-a-horse village owes its existence to the saline water that wells up naturally from the ground. For hundreds of years the water has been diverted down a valley and siphoned into *eras* (saltpans). These are flat evaporation platforms mounted on wooden stilts. It's an eerie sight, rather like the ruins of an ancient Greek city in miniature. As many as 5500 saltpans were still being used in the 1960s but now there are only about 150. The first written reference to salt collection in these parts was in AD 822 but it seems pretty likely that the Romans were at it, too.

There's an attractive church but not much else in the village, which has suffered badly since the decline of the salt pans. The place is more lively during Semana Santa, however, when Judas is put on trial by the villagers. It's something of a kangaroo court; the poor man is always convicted and then burned.

Cañon de Delika

Access from a car park, about 3 km off the A2625, 8 km south of Orduña, signposted 'Monte Santiago'. *Bus: 2 daily to Orduña with La Unión from Vitoria bus station.   Map 6, C3 , inside back cover*

To the west, beyond Salinas and actually reached via the province of Burgos, this spectacular canyon widens to become the valley of Orduña. The River Nervión has its source near here but it's sometimes hard to believe that this is the same river that made Bilbao great, as it's regularly dry in summer. However, when it's in full flow, it spectacularly spills 300 m into the gorge below, creating the highest waterfall in Spain.

There's a good one-and-a-half-hour circular walk from the car park. Follow the right-hand road first, which brings you to the falls, then follow the cliffs to the left, where vultures soar above the valley below. When you reach the second *mirador*, looking down to Orduña, another road descends through beech forest back to the car park. Near here is the **Fuente de Santiago**. Legend has it that St James stopped at this spring to refresh himself and his horse on his journey through Spain.

● *If you're in a car, there's another waterfall to visit on the way back to Vitoria from Orduña. Take the marked side road near the town of Gujuli; the waterfall is prettily set beside a Romanesque church.*

Eastern Alava

The eastern half of the Alava plain is dotted with villages, churches and prehistoric remains. At the northern fringes of the plain, the mountains rise into Guipúzcoa. The town of Salvatierra is the most convenient base for exploration. Part of the Camino de Santiago passes through the natural tunnel of San Adrián here and there's some scenic walking to be done, as well as numerous adventure tourism options (see p211).

▶▶ *See Sleeping p147, Eating and drinking p177*

Salvatierra/Agurain and around

26 km east of Vitoria. *Train: 6 or 7 daily from Vitoria (towards Altsasu or Pamplona), 15 mins, €1.75-2. Map 6, D5, inside back cover*

The main centre in eastern Alava is the not-very-major Salvatierra/Agurain, a well-preserved, walled, medieval town. The sleeping and eating possibilities here are nothing to write home about, although there are a couple of *pensiones*. The helpful tourist office (www.cuadrillasalvatierra.org) is located on the main street, half a block up from the Iglesia de San Juan. The staff hold keys for the churches in Salvatierra, as well as the church at **Gaceo** but currently the only way to visit them is by guided tour (see below).

The area around Salvatierra is notable for its dolmens. Near the village of **Eguilaz**, 45-minutes' walk east of Salvatierra off the N1 is the dolmen of **Aitzkomendi**, discovered by a farmer in 1830. The 11 impressive stones weigh around 10 tonnes and are thought to be early Bronze Age funerary markers. On the other side of Salvatierra near Arrizala is the equally impressive **Sorginetxe** ('house of the witch'), which dates from a similar period. To the east, near the village of Ilarduia, is the **Cueva de Leze**, a huge crevice in the cliff face, 80 m high. It's great for canyoning but access is tricky, so contact a specialist operator, p211.

Iglesias de San Martín, Gaceo, and de la Asunción, Alaiza

Open for 1 hr guided tours only, with Tura T 945-312535, www.tura.org, Tue and Thu or by arrangement, €7 per person (minimum 2 people). Bus: 5 daily Mon-Fri to Gaceo from Vitoria or Salvatierra (destination Araia), 2 daily Sat, 1 daily Sun; there's also a bus to Alaiza from Salvatierra. Map 6, D5, inside back cover

Although current arrangements make access problematic (see Salvatierra), the small village church of **San Martín** in Gaceo is worth the effort. The interior of the 13th-century building is completely covered with impressive frescoes, dating from the 14th century. They were discovered in the 1960s, having been hidden under a hefty coat of plaster. The major scene is a Trinity above the altar, a Crucifixion, and the Last Judgement, with St Michael carefully weighing souls.

Nearby, in the village of Alaiza, the **Iglesia de la Asunción** is also painted but in a bizarrely different, seemingly irreligious style with a childlike technique. It's far from medieval high art but the pictures will be extremely funny to fans of toilet humour!

Túnel de San Adrián and around

Bus: 5 daily to Zalduondo from Vitoria/Salvatierra (destination Araia), 2 daily Sat, 1 daily Sun. Map 6, C5, inside back cover

One of the most interesting walks in the area starts from the hamlet of **Zalduondo**, 8 km north of Salvatierra. The route follows a branch of the Camino de Santiago, the old Roman and medieval highway that effectively linked most of the peninsula with the rest of Europe, and passes through the natural Túnel de San Adrián.

It's about 5.5 km from Zalduondo to a small parking area named Zumarraundi. From there, the track ascends through beech forest to the tunnel. Shortly after the old stone road, there's a right turn up a slope, easily missed: look for the wooden signpost at the top of the rise to your right. The tunnel itself is a spectacular natural cave. It now houses a small chapel, perhaps built to assuage the fears of medieval pilgrims, who thought that the cave was the entrance to Hell. Another anecdote, related with glee by Basques, tells of a Castilian king who travelled eastwards to enforce his rights over Navarra, boasting that he'd never in his life bowed his head or dismounted before any man, least of all Basques. On reaching the low-ceilinged tunnel (with the Navarran deputation smirking on the other side), he wasn't left with much choice…

After the tunnel, the trail continues into Guipúzcoa, reaching the attractive town of **Zegama** after about 90 minutes' walk.

★ Postcard-pretty villages

Best

- Getxo's old port, p57.
- Mundaka, p66.
- Hondarribia, p98.
- Elorrio, p102.
- Laguardia, p116

Los embalses

Bus: 4 daily to Urrúnaga and Legutiano or 3 daily to Ullibarri-Gamboa from Vitoria bus station. Map 6, C4, inside back cover

Not far north of Vitoria, two large artificial lakes help compensate Alavans for the landlocked nature of their province. Brought into existence to supply Vitoria with water, they also serve as popular recreational retreats from the capital. The larger of the two, the Embalse de Urribarri, is more populated, and the place to go for watersports, centred around the pretty town of **Ullibarri-Gamboa**. Urrúnaga, to the west, is most easily accessed from the town of **Legutiano** and has secluded spots, popular with anglers.

Gorbeia

Bus: almost hourly to Murguia from Vitoria station (destination Izarra or Bilbao 'via carretera'). Map 6, B4, inside back cover

Straddling Vizcaya and Alava is the massif of Gorbeia, an enticingly inaccessible area of mountains and gorges topped by the peak of the same name, which hits 1482 m when it remembers not to slouch. It features in Basque consciousness as a realm of deities and purity. There are several good marked trails around Murguia, the principal point of access on the Alava side (20 km northwest of Vitoria), including an ascent of the peak itself, which shouldn't be attempted in poor weather.

La Rioja Alavesa

Basque Rioja? What's this? The two words don't seem to go together but in fact many of the finest Riojas are from Alava province. Confusion reigns because the Spanish province of La Rioja is only one of three that the wine region encompasses. Although it's not far from Vitoria, the Rioja Alavesa definitely feels Spanish rather than Basque; the descent from the green hills into the arid plains crosses a cultural border as well as a geographic one. The hilltop town of Laguardia is one of the most atmospheric places in Euskadi and the surrounding area offers the opportunity to visit some excellent vineyards. The Rioja Alavesa has 200-odd bodegas (the tourist office will provide a complete list), with the majority of winemaking now done outside the old towns in more modern wineries. Phone the wineries in advance to organize a visit; the larger your group, the better your chance of a warm welcome.

The surrounding area also has a few non-vinous attractions and a series of marked walking and cycling routes, spectacularly backed by the Sierra Cantábrica. If you're coming from Vitoria by car, it's marginally quicker and certainly more scenic to head south on the A-2124/A-124 rather than take the Logroño motorway. After ascending to a pass, the high ground dramatically drops away to the Riojan plain and there's a superb lookout known as El Balcón (the balcony).

▸▸ *See Sleeping p148, Eating and drinking p178*

★ Laguardia/Biasteri

45 km from Vitoria. *Bus: 3 or 4 daily with Continental from Vitoria bus station. Map 6, E4, inside back cover*

The small walled hilltop town of Laguardia, with a population of just 1500, stands at an altitude of 1500 feet and commands the plain like a sentinel. This is no accident: the town was originally called La Guardia de Navarra, the 'guard of Navarra'.

The town itself is captivating. Founded in 1164, its narrow medieval streets are lovely to wander around and, lurking beneath like catacombs, are over 300 small cellars or *bodegas*, used for the making and storing of wine and as a place to hide in troubled times. The impressive **Iglesia de Santa María de los Reyes** (*tours Sat and Sun 1730 and 1830, €2; at other times keys are available at the tourist office*) was begun in the 12th century and has a finely preserved painted Gothic façade. The former **Ayuntamiento** on Plaza Nueva was inaugurated in the 16th century.

Laguardia was the birthplace of the writer of fables Felix de Samaniego. His family was the richest in town and their large residence is now divided between the tourist office and **Bodega El Fabulista** (Pl San Juan s/n, **T** 945-621192. *Tours daily 1130, 1300 and 1730, €5*), one of the few *bodegas* that is still in use. A massive contrast to Palacio (see below), which produces two million bottles a year, Bodega El Fabulista is run, almost singlehandedly, by its owner, Eusebio, and produces about 40,000 bottles a year. The wines, marketed as *Decidido*, are good young-drinking reds and whites and are made in the underground cellar from grapes Eusebio grows himself, using very traditional methods. Guided tours of the *bodega* are excellent and include lots of background information on the Rioja wine region, as well as a generous tasting in a beautiful underground vault. The tours are in Spanish but English and French guides can be arranged with advance notice; in fact, it's still worth doing the tour in Spanish just to have a look and a taste!

● *A set of small lakes near Laguardia is one of Spain's better spots for birdwatching, particularly from September to March when migrating species abound.*

Bodegas Palacio

Ctra de Elciego s/n, Laguardia, **T** 945-600057/945-5621195, www.cosmepalacio.com. *Tours Tue-Sun 1230 and 1330, €3 (redeemable in shop or restaurant); booking essential.*

One of the easiest wineries to get to is Bodegas Palacio, located just below Laguardia on the Elciego road, a 10-minute walk from

Cutting a swathe through the surrounding vineyards, Bodegas Ysios was designed by Santiago Calatrava to echo the Alavan landscape.

town. The winery is modern but the older *bodega* alongside has been charmingly converted into a hotel and restaurant. Palacio produces a range of wines, the quality of which has improved over recent years. Their *Glorioso* and *Cosme Palacio* labels are widely sold in the UK. Until recently it was owned by the Canadian multinational *Seagrams*, so it is well geared to visitors and runs informative daily tours (which must be booked by phone). The tours are in Spanish but English guides are available.

The winery was originally founded in 1894 and is fairly typical of the area, producing 90% red wine from the Tempranillo grape and 10% white from Viura. The altitude here means that the grapes ripen slowly and the vintage is in the first week of October. As well as *crianzas*, *reservas* and *gran reservas* (see p120), Palacio also produces a soft, fruity red wine for drinking young, which is a change from the heavier Rioja styles. The tour improves after the initial video and you get the chance to taste a couple of the wines.

● *Palacio runs monthly tasting weekends for €300 for two people, including two nights in the hotel, a tasting session and some meals.*

La Hoya

2 km north of Laguardia. Oct-Apr Tue-Sat 1100-1500, Sun 1000-1400; May-Sep Tue-Fri 1100-1400, 1600-2000, Sat 1100-1500, Sun 1000-1400. Free. Map 6, E4, inside back cover

The Iron Age settlement of **La Hoya** near Laguardia was founded in about 1100 BC. There's a small museum at the site. Extensively settled in prehistoric times, the area also has numerous dolmens, some within walking distance of Laguardia. The best, **Hechicera**, is 6 km to the east, near Elvillar and dates from about 2100 BC.

Herederos del Marqués de Riscal

*C Torrea 1, Elciego, **T** 945 606000 (Mon-Fri), www.marquesderiscal.com. Bus: 3 or 4 daily between Vitoria and Logroño stop in Elciego and Laguardia, 7 km away. Map 6, F4, inside back cover*

Founded in 1860, Marqués de Riscal is the oldest and best known of the Rioja *bodegas* and has built a formidable reputation for the quality of its wines. The Marqués himself was a Madrid journalist who, having cooled off in France after getting in some hot political water at home, started making wine on his return to Spain. Enlisting the help of Monsieur Pinot, a French expert, he experimented by planting Cabernet Sauvignon, which is still used today.

The winery is modern but remains faithful to the *bodega's* rigorous tradition of quality. The historic collection of Riscal wines includes some bottles from as far back as 1862. As well as the traditionally elegant *reserva* and *gran reserva*, the more recently inaugurated *Baron de Chirel* is a very classy red indeed, coming from low-yielding old vines and exhibiting more French character than is typical of the region.

▶ Wine

In good Catholic fashion, wine is the blood of Spain. It's the standard accompaniment to most meals but also features very prominently in bars, where a glass of cheap *tinto* or *blanco* can cost as little as €0.30, although it's normally more.

The two principal wine denominations in the Basque lands are *txakolí*, produced near the coast between Bilbao and San Sebastián; and Rioja, one of whose three regions lies in Alava, south of Vitoria.

Txakolí (chacolí) has a small production which was awarded DO status (*Denominación de Origen*, similar to the French *appelation controlée*) in 1990. The most common form is a young, refreshing, acidic white, with a green tinge and a slight sparkle, often accentuated by pouring from a height. The best examples, from around Getaria, go beautifully with seafood. Made from under-ripe grapes of the Ondarrubi Zuria variety; there's also a less common red and rosé.

The overall standard of Riojas has improved markedly since the granting of the higher DOC status in 1991, involving stringent testing. The Basque section, the Rioja Alavesa, produces many of the region's best wines, which are mostly fullish-bodied reds from the Tempranillo grape (with three other permitted red grapes often used to add depth or character). Whites from Viura and Malvasia are also produced: the majority of these are young, fresh and dry, unlike those powerful oaky Rioja whites sold in the UK. Rosés are also produced.

The quality of individual Riojas varies widely according to both the producer and the amount of time the wines have been aged in oak barrels and in the bottle: the words *crianza*, *reserva* and *gran reserva* all refer to the length of the aging process. The vintage date is also indicated on the bottle.

Among other regions, neighbouring Navarra produces

some quality wines unfettered by the stricter rules governing Rioja production. The Ribera del Duero region, meanwhile, has been building a reputation for red wines of the highest quality. It's been dubbed the 'Spanish Burgundy' and the description isn't altogether misplaced; the better wines have the rich nose and delicate earthy quality of the better reds from that area. Rueda, around Valladolid, produces some excellent dry whites from the Verdejo and Viura grapes. In many bars, you can order Ribera, Rueda or other regions by the glass but note that if you ask for 'crianza' or 'reserva', you'll get a Rioja.

Crianza: A red *crianza* must be at least two years old and have spent six months in oak (12 in the case of Rioja).

Reserva: A red *reserva* must have passed its third birthday and spent 12 months (often more) in oak.

Gran Reserva: This is the softest and most characterful of the Riojas, although it sometimes tends to be overaged. It must be at least five years old, including two or more years in oak. It is only produced in good years.

Cosechero: A young red usually produced by carbonic maceration, where the whole grapes begin to ferment in carbon dioxide before being pressed. This gives a fruity, slightly fizzy wine – a good match for many of the region's hearty foods.

Vino Corriente/Normal/de Mesa: The cheap option in bars and restaurants. Table wine which can vary from terrible to reasonable. It's often high in acid, which balances the oily Spanish food. Served in a tumbler in bars so there's no pretending.

Fresco: Most bars keep a bottle of red 'fresco', or chilled; a refreshing hot weather option.

Kalimotxo: The drink of choice for students: red wine mixed 50/50 with Coca-Cola. Often served in *kutxis*, paper cups holding a litre that are nursed solo or shared with straws.

Vino Generoso: Generous, ie fortified, wine, such as sherry.

The winery's innovative spirit continues to this day. Marqués de Riscal has enlisted Frank Gehry to design its new visitors' complex, which will include a hotel, restaurant, exhibition centre and other facilities. Due to open in summer 2006, Gehry's building (a model of which is displayed at the *bodega*) incorporates ribbons of coloured titanium over a building of natural stone. The silver, gold, and 'dusty rose' sheets are Gehry's response to "the unbroken landscape of vineyards and rich tones". For the moment the *bodega* welcomes interested visitors by prior appointment only and it's usually essential to reserve several weeks in advance.

● *Elciego is a pleasant little village with a hotel and the chunkily beautiful church of San Andrés, which has one massive arched nave.*

Bodegas Ysios
Camino de la Hoya s/n, 2 km north of Laguardia. **T** 945-600640.
Map 6, E4, inside back cover

North of Laguardia is Bodegas Ysios *bodega*, designed by Santiago Calatrava, the Valencian engineer/architect who has made the Basque country his second home. The waved design echoes the steep mountains. The winery produces quality *reservas* made from pure Tempranillo and aged in French oak.

Oyon/Oion
Bus: 7 or 8 daily with Autoyón from Logroño, which is easily reached by several daily buses from Laguardia. *Map 6, F5, inside back cover*

Twenty minutes east of Laguardia is the pretty but parched town of Oyon/Oion. One of the bigger wine operations here is **Bodegas Faustino Martínez** (**T** 945-622500). It runs a good in-depth tour in Spanish or English but bear in mind that it's not as geared to visitors as might be expected and there's no tasting at the end. Oyon has an excellent restaurant, Mesón La Cueva, which serves a good lunch *menú* in its airy new upstairs dining room (see p178).

The standard of accommodation in the Basque country is very high: even the most modest *pensión* is usually very clean and respectable. Places to stay (*alojamientos*) are divided into three main categories: *hoteles* (marked H or HR) are graded from one to five stars, while *hostales* (Hs or HsR) – not hostels! – also have a star-rating system. The difference between *hoteles* and *hostales* is complex and there's significant crossover. *Pensiones* (P) are the standard budget option and are usually family-run flats in an apartment block. An excellent alternative, if you have transport, is the network of *agroturismos* and *casas rurales*. The best of these are traditional Basque farmhouses. Many are in picturesque settings and most offer exceptional value. While some are listed in this section, the tourist offices in the region will provide you with a booklet listing all of them. There are a few official youth hostels in the Basque region but the price of *pensiones* rarely makes it worth the trouble except for solo travellers. They are frequently populated by noisy schoolkids and have curfews and check-out times.

Sleeping codes

Most campsites in the Basque country are on the coast and are set up as well-equipped villages for holidaying families. In other areas, camping, unless specifically prohibited, is a matter of common sense: most locals will know of (or offer) a place where you can pitch a tent *tranquilamente*.

Bilbao/Bilbo

Casco Viejo
Metro: Casco Viejo, Tram: Arriaga, unless otherwise stated.

AL Barceló Hotel Avenida, Av Zumalacárregui 40, **T** 944-124300, **F** 944-114617. *No tram.   Map 3, A6, p252* Five minutes from the top exit of the Casco Viejo metro, on the hilltop above the old town, this business-oriented hotel has 143 rooms and great panoramic views of the city.

AL Hotel Tryp Arenal, C Fueros 2, **T** 944-153100, **F** 944-156395, tryp.arenal@solmelia.com. *Map 5, C2, p 256* In a colourful building on the edge of the Casco Viejo, this is a comfortable chain hotel with well-appointed doubles and slightly cramped singles. Spick and span, it offers significantly cheaper weekend rates.

A Petit Palace Arana, C Bidebarrieta 2, **T** 944-156411, **F** 944-161205, www.hthoteles.com. *Map 5, B2, p256* With an unbeatable location on the edge of the Casco Viejo, this beautiful building has been very sensitively converted into a smart modern hotel, with a pretty upstairs breakfast room. There's free internet access for guests and the best of the rooms have a computer terminal and exercise bike. There are good-value, innovative family suites with fold-down beds, and rooms equipped for the disabled. Book on the internet for the best rates. The closest parking is under the Plaza Nueva.

B Hotel Bilbao Jardines, C Jardines 9, **T** 944-794210, www.hotelbilbaojardines.com. *Map 5, E2, p256* Right in the heart of the Casco Viejo *pintxo* zone, this newly opened hotel is an attractive option at a fair price. The rooms have a stripped-back, comfortable feel, with light-wood floorboards. The best are on the top floor, with sloping ceilings. The management is very friendly.

B-C Hotel Sirimiri, Pl de la Encarnación 3, **T** 944-330759, **F** 944-330875, www.hotelsirimiri.com. *Tram: Atxuri. Map 5, F6, p256* Named after the light misty rain that is a feature of the city, this is a gem of a hotel in a quiet square. The genial owner has equipped it with a gym and sauna and there is free parking available. Rooms come with TV, heating and telephone.

C Hostal Mardones, C Jardines 4, **T** 944-153105, www.hostal mardones.com. *Map 5, E2, p256* Situated in *pintxo* heartland and entered by the side of a newsstand, this *hostal* is fitted in attractive dark wood. Both exterior and interior rooms are pleasant, light, airy and have been recently refurbished, with modern bathrooms and wireless internet access. The owner is welcoming and chatty.

★ **Best**

Pensiones with a bit of charm

- Iturrienea Ostatua, Casco Viejo, Bilbao, p127.
- Pensión Ladero, Casco Viejo, Bilbao, p128.
- Hostal Itxas-Gain, Getaria, p138.
- Pensión Gran Bahía, Parte Vieja, San Sebastián, p139.
- Pensión Amaiur, Parte Vieja, San Sebastián, p139.

C Hotel Arriaga, C Ribera 3, **T** 944-790001, **F** 944-790516, www.hotel arriaga.org. *Map 5, D1, p256* This is a very friendly, good-value hotel with excellent rooms that feature floor-to-ceiling windows and views over the theatre. Decoration and fittings are plush and formal. There's parking underneath for €12 per night; it's the only hotel in the old quarter with its own garage.

C Iturrienea Ostatua, C Santa María, **T** 944-161500, **F** 944-158929. *Map 5, E2, p256* This beautiful *pensión* is lovingly fitted out in stone and wood, and decorated with idiosyncratic objects. With its delicious breakfasts and homely rooms, you might want to move in. This is one of Bilbao's most charming and central choices, so book well in advance. Recommended.

D Hostal La Estrella, C María Muñoz 6, **T** 944-164066, www.hostallaestrella.com. *Map 5, D4, p256* A reasonable if overpriced option that has seen slightly better days, but has spacious rooms with or without bathroom, all-night access, and a bar. The rooms with balcony are nice, but can be noisy in the mornings.

D Hostal Roquefer, C Lotería 2, **T** 944-150755. *Map 5, E3 p256* This is a last resort and usually the last place to fill up. Some of the rooms are quite pleasant but others are shabby and stuffy, so make sure you see a few before committing. Overpriced.

D/E Hostal Gurea, C Bidebarrieta 14, **T** 944-163299. *Map 5, E2, p256* A carefully refurbished and well-scrubbed establishment on one of Casco Viejo's principal streets, Gurea has rooms both with and without bathroom. The owners are welcoming and cheerfully vague about bookings but usually request a 0100 curfew.

D/E Hostal Méndez, C Santa María 13, **T** 944-160364, www.pensionmendez.com. *Map 5, E2, p256* A dignified building with castle-sized doors and iron guard dogs at the entrance. The first floor has *hostal*-grade rooms with new bathrooms. The fourth floor is *pensión*-style: simple but adequate. Many rooms have balconies.

E Pensión Ladero, C Lotería 1, **T** 944-150932, www.pension ladero.com. *Map 5, E3, p256* Right in the thick of things, this small and welcoming option has cork tiles, good shared bathrooms and very well-priced rooms, with TV, some of which are reached by a tiny spiral staircase. There's a hearty Basque welcome guaranteed; just as well, as it's on the fourth floor with no lift. Excellent value. Recommended. No bookings.

F Pensión Manoli, C Libertad 2, **T** 944-155636. *Map 5, C3, p256* In the heart of the Casco Viejo, Manoli is bright and well maintained. The good-value exterior rooms have balconies and shared facilities.

Riverbank

L Barceló Hotel Nervión, C Paseo Campo Volantín 11, **T** 944-454700, **F** 944-455608, www.barcelonervion.com. *Metro: Casco Viejo, Tram: Uribitarte. Map 4, A10, p255* The cavernous lobby of this modish luxury hotel includes a piano that is the focus of a weekly jazz session. The well-designed rooms offer all the expected comforts, including the business traveller's delight, Playstation. Some rooms have good river views.

L Gran Domine, Alameda Mazarredo 61, **T** 944-211198. **F** 253301, www.granhoteldomine.com. *Tram: Guggenheim. Map 1, C6, p254*
This modern five-star hotel is opposite the Guggenheim and has been designed with the same innovation and levity in mind. The façade consists of 48 mirrors at slightly different angles, while the delightful interior is dominated by a large central atrium. The rooms with Guggenheim views cost a little more but are worth it. There's also a good bar and restaurant. Inspiring and recommended.

L Miróhotel Bilbao, Alameda Mazarredo 77, **T** 946-611880, **F** 902-117755, www.mirohotelbilbao.com. *Tram: Guggenheim Map 4, D6, p254* Also close to the Guggenheim and enjoying some great views of the museum, this is a sleek hotel with a Catalan touch: both architect Carmen Abad and interior designer Antonio Miró hail from Barcelona. It's impressively modern, with touches of whimsy. The rooms are spacious and have a Nordic feel, thanks to the white fittings. Rates vary substantially according to when and how you book; you may get better deals from an online dealer or travel agent than from the hotel's own website. Facilities are extensive and include a jacuzzi and a stylish bar. Staff are helpful and friendly.

C Hostal Begoña, C Amistad 2, **T** 944-230134, **F** 944-230133, www.hostalbegona.com. *Metro: Abando. Map 4, C12, p255*
A refit has transformed the Begoña into a welcoming modern hotel, packed with flair and comfort. From the inviting library and lounge to the large chalet-style rooms and mini-suites at very reasonable prices, this is an excellent option. The hotel offers free internet, and the friendly boss can help organize trips around Euskadi, including a range of outdoor activities. Recommended.

D Pensión Bilbao, C Amistad 2, **T** 944-246943, **F** 944-352426. *Metro: Abando. Map 4, C12, p255* Neat rooms with bath in a refurbished building just across the river from Casco Viejo. The small exterior rooms have balconies with geraniums in window boxes.

El Ensanche

LL Hotel Carlton, Pl Moyúa 2, **T** 944-162200, **F** 944-164628, www.aranzazu-hoteles.com. *Metro: Moyúa. Map 4, E8, p255* This grand old hotel, set in the centre of the Ensanche on noisy Plaza Moyúa, is considerably more luxurious inside than out. Its refurbished neo-classical ambience has accommodated Einstein, Lorca and Hemingway among other notables.

LL Hotel López de Haro, C Obispo Orueta 2, **T** 944-235500, **F** 234500, www.hotellopezdeharo.com. *Metro: Moyúa. Map 4, C9, p255* A modern but characterful five-star hotel in classic style. Although there are better value hotels in town, it's deservedly popular for its genuinely helpful service and excellent restaurant. Check the website for special deals.

L Hotel Ercilla, C Ercilla 37-39, **T** 944-705700, **F** 944-439335, www.hotelercilla.es. *Metro: Indautxu. Map 4, G7, p255* Well located on the city's main shopping street, this four-star hotel has been newly renovated and is much the better for it. With quality service and a busy, metropolitan feel, it makes an excellent base, and is well priced for the amenities on offer. There are excellent weekend rates, with savings up to 40%. Check the website for current offers. The hotel restaurant, *Bermeo* (see p155), is one of Bilbao's best.

L Hotel Indautxu, Pl Bombero Etxariz s/n, **T** 944-211198, **F** 944-221331, www.hoteles-silken.com. *Metro: Indautxu. Map 4, H8, p255* Behind a mirrored façade, which bizarrely dwarfs the older building in front, comfortable executive-style rooms overlook a comparatively quiet square. Pianists make the odd scheduled appearance in the bar and there's an outside terrace. It has bags more character than the average business hotel and is cheerfully run.

L Hotel Jardines de Albia, C San Vicente 6, **T** 944-354140, **F** 354142, www.husa.es. *Metro: Abando. Map 4, C10, p255* Fronted by a mermaid and set in a peaceful back street near the gardens after which it is named, this is another upmarket hotel that offers substantial weekend discounts. Fairly attractively furnished, the rooms are more homely than might be expected. There's a spa and hydrotherapy centre in the building.

AL Hotel Hesperia Zubialde, Camino de la Ventosa 34, **T** 944-008100, **F** 944-008110, www.hesperia-zubialde.com. *Metro: San Mamés, Tram: Sabino Arana. Map 4, H3, p254* This is the nicest of the cluster of hotels catering for the trade fair and congress centre. In a detached restored building away from the downtown bustle, it's modern and efficient but pleasant. There's a terrace café and a very reasonably priced restaurant. The hotel also boasts sweeping views over the maritime museum, the river and Deusto.

B Hotel Zabálburu, C Pedro Martínez Artola 8, **T** 944-437100, **F** 944-100073, www.hotelzabalburu.com. *Euskotren: Zabálburu. Map 4, H10, p255* Although not in the most attractive part of Bilbao, this family-run hotel is comfortable and promises attentive service. Prices are cheaper off-season and parking is available for €8 per day.

C Hotel Vista Alegre, C Pablo Picasso 13, **T** 944-431450, **F** 944-431454, www.hotelvistaalegre.com. *Euskotren: Zabálburu. Map 4, H11, p255* An atmospheric if faded hotel near the bullring, with lots of old Basque prints, a certain stuffy plushness and considerate staff. It's pretty good value year-round.

D Hostal Central, Alameda Rekalde 35, **T** 944-106339, **F** 944-701576, www.hostalcentral.com. *Metro: Moyúa. Map 4, F8, p254* True to its name, this newish option is right in the centre of the city, a block from Plaza Moyúa in prime shopping territory. The rooms are colourful, attractive and pretty good value. There's a pleasant feeling about the place: the staff are very much at home with tourists and are helpful with information. Internet access and wireless network available.

G Albergue Bilbao Aterpetxea, Ctra Basurto-Kastrexana 70, **T** 944-270054, **F** 944-275479, http://albergue.bilbao.net. *Bus 58 from Pl Circular and the bus station.* Bilbao's HI hostel is a vast structure by a motorway on the outskirts of Bilbao. Despite its inconvenient location, it does have good facilities (including bike hire), although it is often overrun with school groups. It's just about the cheapest bed in town for single travellers (around €13.50 per person depending on season) but couples won't save much and the 0930 check-out is a shock to the system. There's a dining room with full meal service but no kitchen.

Deusto/Deustu

A NH Hotel de Deusto, C Francisco Maciá 9, **T** 944-760006, **F** 944-762199, www.nh-hotels.com. *Metro: Deustu, Tram: Abandoibarra. Map 4, D2, p254* This colourfully decorated hotel is an enjoyable place to stay on this side of the river. The large rooms feature minibar, safe, Playstation and inviting beds. Downstairs is an attractively arty bar and restaurant.

C Hotel Artetxe, Camino de Berriz 112, **T** 944-747780, **F** 944-746020, www.hotel-artetxe.com. High above Deusto on the Artxanda ridge, this renovated farmhouse offers superb views over the whole city. It has attractive wooden furnishings and small but homely bedrooms with beams and views. It's a great place to stay but not that handy for access to Bilbao without a car. There's a good traditional-style restaurant here too.

D Hotel Plaza San Pedro, C Luzarra 7, **T** 944-763126, **F** 944-763895, www.hplazasanpedro.com. *Metro: Deustu. Map 4, D1, p254*

Somewhat disconcertingly set on a back street of vehicle workshops and down-to-earth wine bars, this hotel is pretty close to the centre of Deusto life, attractively modern and well priced.

Getxo and around

AL Gran Hotel Puente Colgante, C María Díaz de Haro 2, **T** 944-014800, **F** 944-014810, www.granhotelpuentecolgante.com. *Euskotren: Portugalete.* In a renovated 19th-century building with a grand façade, this upmarket hotel is superbly situated right next to the Puente Vizcaya. All the rooms face outwards and have good mattresses and a restrained elegance. The hotel has a decent range of facilities. It's a short train ride into the centre of Bilbao.

A Hotel Los Tamarises, Muelle de Ereaga 2, **T** 944-910005, **F** 944-911310. *Metro: Neguri.* Another beachfront option, this is not as pretty as the Igeretxe but has considerably plusher rooms and similarly good views. There's a huge café-restaurant with a terrace that's a prime Getxo meeting point in summer.

B Hotel Neguri, Algortako Etorbidea 14, **T** 944-910509. *Metro: Neguri.* On the main road, this boutique hotel has seen sprucer days but it's charming and refreshingly un-businessy.

C Hotel Igeretxe, Playa de Ereaga s/n, **T** 944-910009, **F** 944-608599. *Metro: Neguri.* Shaded by palms, this welcoming hotel is right on Ereaga beach, Getxo's main social strand. Formerly a *balneario*, the hotel still offers some spa facilities, as well as a restaurant overlooking the slightly grubby sand. Breakfast included.

D Pensión Usategi, C Landene 2, **T** 944-913918. *Metro: Bidezabal.* Well placed on the headland above Arrigunaga beach, Usategi has clean, cool rooms, some of which have great views.

E Pensión Areeta, C Mayor 13 (Las Arenas), **T** 944-638136.
Metro: Areeta. Near the metro of the same name and a stone's
throw from the Puente Vizcaya, this is a good place in the heart of
the trendy Las Arenas district of Getxo.

Camping Sopelana, Ctra Bilbao-Plentzia s/n, **T** 946-762120.
Metro: Sopelana. Very handy for the Metro into Bilbao, this is the
most convenient campsite within range of the city and is close to
the Getxo shops and beach, too. Sopelana is well-equipped and
also has reasonable value bungalows available.

Basque coastline

Bermeo, Mundaka and around

A Hotel Atalaya, C Itxaropen 1, Mundaka, **T** 946-177000,
F 946-876899, www.hotel-atalaya-mundaka.com. The classiest
of the town's options, with a summery feel to its rooms, some of
which have excellent views. Garden and parking adjoin the stately
building. Good service and nice breakfasts.

B-C Hotel El Puerto, Portu Kalea 1, Mundaka, **T** 946-876725,
F 946-876726, hotelelpuerto@euskalnet.net. The best value of
Mundaka's three hotels is set right by the tiny fishing harbour and
has delightfully cosy rooms; those overlooking the water are worth
the few extra euros. The bar below is also highly recommended.

C Hostal Torre Ercilla, C Talaranzko 14, Bermeo, **T** 946-187598,
F 946-884231, barrota@piramidal.com. A lovely place to stay in
Bermeo's old town, between the museum and the church.
The rooms are thoughtfully designed for relaxation, with small
balconies, reading nooks and soft carpet. There's also a lounge,
terrace, chessboard and barbecue, among other comforts.

C Hotel Arimune, C Bentalde 95, Bakio, **T** 946-194022. Right on the beach in Bakio, a *txakolí*-producing town between Bilbao and Bermeo. The hotel façade is strewn with cheery honeysuckle and the interior is more originally decorated than many beach hotels. The terrace is a peaceful spot out of peak season. Closed Dec-Feb.

Camping Portuondo, 1 km out of Mundaka on the road to Gernika, **T/F** 946-877701, www.campingportuondo.com. Packed like a sardine tin during the summer months, this is a well-equipped campsite with a swimming pool, café and laundry. The bungalows, with kitchen, fridge and television, sleep up to four but are not significantly cheaper than the hotels in town.

Gernika and around

A Hotel Katxi, Morga/Andra Mari s/n, **T** 946-270740, **F** 946-270245. A few kilometres west of Gernika in the hamlet of Morga is this excellent rural hotel. The rooms, some larger than others, are extremely comfortable and there's a friendly lounge area. It's a great place to get away from things a little, in a warm atmosphere. The same owners run a good *asador* next door.

B Hotel Gernika, C Carlos Gangoiti 17, **T** 946-254948, **F** 946-255874, www.hotel-gernika.com. Gernika's best hotel is nothing exceptional, set in a nondescript brick building on the edge of town. However, the rooms are comfortable, if uninteresting, and there's a bar and café. Service is helpful.

C Pensión Akelarre, C Barrenkale 5, **T** 946-270197, **F** 946-270675. A funky little place in the heart of the pedestrian area. Rooms have TV and stripped floorboards and there's a sunny terrace. Discounts are available if you stay for more than one night and it's significantly cheaper off-season.

E Bizketxe, Oma 8, near Gernika, **T** 946-254906, **F** 946-255573. If you've got your own transport, this is an great place to stay, located in the perfect Basque hamlet of Oma, underneath the painted wood. Lovely rooms in a traditional farmhouse, with or without bath.

E Pensión Madariaga, C Industria 10, **T** 946-256035. Very attractively furnished little place. The welcoming rooms offer TV, bathroom and decent furniture for not a great deal of cash.

Ugaldebarri, **T/F** 946-256577, elenaelan@euskalnet.net. Located on the eastern side of the estuary, with superb views over the reserve, this farmhouse is rented out as a whole and has two double rooms. If you're a family with transport, it's an excellent place to stay. €80 per day in summer and €50 at other times.

Lekeitio

C Emperatriz Zita, Santa Elena Etorbidea s/n, **T** 946-842655, **F** 946-243500, www.aisiahoteles.com. This slightly odd-looking hotel was built on the site of a palace where Empress Zita lived in the 1920s. Married to the last Austro-Hungarian emperor, she was left with eight children when he died of pneumonia on Madeira in 1922. The hotel is furnished in suitably elegant style and is a thalasso-therapy (seawater treatment) and health centre. The rooms and restaurant are well-priced, considering their location and quality.

B Hotel Zubieta, Portal de Atea, **T** 946-843030, **F** 946-841099, www.hotelzubieta.com A superbly converted coachhouse in the grounds of a *palacio*. Considering its surprisingly low prices and friendly management, this is one of the best places to stay. There's a lively bar and cosy rooms, with sloping wooden ceilings. Light sleepers, however, will enjoy it more at weekends, as the timber yard next door can be noisy on weekday mornings. The hotel also has reasonably priced two- and four-person apartments. Recommended.

D Piñupe Hotela, Av Pascual Abaroa 10, **T** 946-842984, **F** 946-840772. The cheapest place in town, and a sound choice. The rooms are en suite with phone and TV, and are much more comfortable than the bar downstairs would suggest.

Markina

D/E Hotel Vega, C Abasua 2, **T** 946-166015. This sleepy place on the square is a relaxing base and has rooms both with and without bathroom. There's a popular café with a terrace downstairs.

Monte Baserria, Barrio Arta 23, near Bolibar, **T** 944-130987, 606-255424 (mobile). This big house, attractively furnished in a rustic style, can be rented for a weekend or by the week. It sleeps up to seven people and costs €120-130 per night, making it good value for a group. It's a good base for walking in the surrounding area.

Ondarroa

D/E Arrigorri, Arrigorri 3, **T** 946-134045, **F** 946-833307. A good option across the river from the centre of Ondarroa, perched right over the beach. There are a variety of rooms at differing prices; the best have sea views. Friendly and comfortable. Breakfast included.

F Patxi, Arta Bide 21, **T** 609-986446 (mobile). An exceedingly low-priced *pensión* that has colourful and comfortable rooms with a basic shared bathroom.

Guipúzcoan coast

C-D Pensión Iribar, C Nagusia 34, Getaria, **T** 943-140406. Right in the heart of the old town, around the back of the restaurant of the same name, are clean and comfy modern rooms with bathroom.

D Gure Ametsa, Orrua s/n, Getaria, **T** 943-140077.   Off a backroad between Zumaia and Getaria, this friendly farmhouse is in a superb location, with views out to sea. Cheaper rooms do not have en suite bathrooms.

D Pensión Txikipolit, Pl Musica s/n, Zarautz, **T** 943-835357, **F** 943-833731.   One of the best budget options, very well located in the old part of town. Comfy rooms, with character; some of the cheaper ones do not have private bathrooms.

E Hostal Itxas-Gain, C San Roque 1, Getaria, **T** 943-141033. A lovely, warm-hearted place, overlooking the sea, with charming rooms. On the top floor there's a suite with a spa-bath. There's also a garden, which is a top place to chill in hot weather, and a friendly dog. Open Easter-September.

San Sebastián/Donostia

All accommodation in San Sebastián is overpriced. High season is June to September; prices are at least 30% lower outside this period. The old town is bristling with more than 30 *pensiones*, and there are several good *agroturismos* in the hills behind San Sebastián; contact the tourist office for a complete list.

Parte Vieja

AL Hotel Parma, C General Jauregui 11, **T** 943-428893, **F** 943-424082, www.hotelparma.com. *Map 2, A5, p250*   A fairly bland modern hotel whose happiest features are its location by the river mouth and the views of the Kursaal from the better rooms.

B-C Pensión Edorta, C Puerto 15, **T** 943-423773, www.pension edorta.com. *Map 2, B3, p250*   Overpriced but charming, this lovely *pensión* is right in the old town near the fishing harbour. Only recently opened, it has beautiful rooms, with rough stone-faced walls, polished floorboards and elegant iron headed beds. The bathrooms, too, are very stylish, but some of them are shared.

B-D Pensión Gran Bahía, C Embeltrán 16, **T** 943 420216, www.paisvasco.com/granbahia. *Map 2, B4, p250* This upmarket *pensión* is very convenient for both the beach and the Parte Vieja. The renovated rooms are well-equipped and quiet, with en suite bathrooms, heating, air conditioning and very comfortable beds.

B-D Pensión Itxasoa, C San Juan 14, **T/F** 943-420132, itxasoa @pensionesconencanto.com. *Map 2, A4, p250* This well-located and attractively decorated *pensión* has great views over the river mouth and out to sea. Staff are helpful and welcoming.

C-E Pensión Anne, C Esterlines 15, **T** 943-421438, www.pension anne.com. *Map 2, B4, p250* Behind an imposing wooden door is a spotlessly bright, welcoming *pensión*. All rooms are exterior, with heating, TV and optional bathroom. It's got an arty, homely feel and is good value outside the summer months. Recommended.

C-E Pensión San Jerónimo, C San Jerónimo 25, **T** 943-427525, www.pensionsanjeronimo.com. *Map 2, B3, p250* This spick-and-span place is ideally situated right in the heart of the old town and offers better value than many. The rooms have shiny wooden floors and the beds, if on the small side, are new and firm. All rooms have a small bathroom.

D-E Pensión Amaiur, C 31 de Agosto 44, **T** 943-429654, www.pensionamaiur.com. *Map 2, B3, p250* The oldest surviving house in the Parte Vieja (few others survived the 1813 fire) has some of the best budget rooms in town. Lovingly decorated and sympathetically run, most have satellite TV, some have balconies. There's also a (stoveless) kitchen and high-speed internet access.

D-E Pensión Larrea, C Narrica 21, **T** 943-422694. *Map 2, B4, p250* A well-situated *pensión* with cheerful management. The rooms are all exterior, with small balconies, and the shared bathrooms are clean. Prices are often negotiable.

D-F Pensión San Lorenzo, C San Lorenzo 2, **T** 943-425516, www.pensionsanlorenzo.com. *Map 2, B4, p250* A friendly star of the old town near the Bretxa market. The five well-priced rooms are not only brightly decorated but come with TV, fridge, kettle, piped radio and bathroom. There's also internet access at €2 per hour; the first 15 minutes are complimentary. It's a quiet place and is highly recommended but it fills up very fast. The San Lorenzo's sister set-up, **Pensión Boulevard** (Alameda del Boulevard 24, **T** 943- 429405, *Map 2, B4, p250*) is more expensive (**C**) and not quite as homely but has four cared-for rooms, with bathroom, TV and fridge.

Centro and new town

LL Hotel Londres y Inglaterra, C Zubieta 2, **T** 943-440770, **F** 943-440491, www.hlondres.com. *Map 2, E4, p250* Grand old beachfront hotel that is an emblem of the city's glory days. Great location and good service. If royalty don't drop by as often as they once did, no one is letting on.

LL Hotel María Cristina, C Oquendo 1, **T** 943-437600, **F** 943-437676, www.westin.com/mariacristina. *Map 2, C5, p250* A riverfront hotel that may be difficult to spot – if you're in orbit. Taking up an entire block, its sandstone bulk has cradled a stellar cast of celebrities. It has all the facilities and style you would expect, including a childminding service and a proper concierge, as well as prices that boot other Basque hotels into campsite class.

AL Hotel Niza, C Zubieta 56, **T** 943-426663, **F** 943-441251, www.hotelniza.com. *Map 2, F3, p250* Slap bang on the beach, this hotel is an odd mixture of seaside casualness and starchy formality. About half the rooms have views; it goes without saying that these are better than the others, some of which are noisy.

B Hostal Alemana, C San Martín 53, **T** 943-462544, **F** 943- 461771, www.hostalalemana.com. *Map 2, F3, p250* An efficient modern hotel with warm personal service. Despite its *hostal* category it has all the conveniences of a hotel, plus some nice views and a pretty breakfast room. Minimum five-night stay in August.

B Pensión Bellas Artes, C Urbieta 64, **T** 943-474905, www.pension-bellasartes.com. *Map 2, G5, p251* A well-run, nicely decorated *pensión* near the Euskotren station. Rooms are delightfully cosy and atmospheric.

C Pensión San Martín, C San Martín 10, **T** 943-428714. *Map 2, E5, p250* One of the better choices of many on this street. The comfortable rooms have bathrooms and TV. The location is very handy for the train station, if you've got heavy bags.

D Pensión Urkia, C Urbieta 12, **T** 943-428123; **Pensión La Perla**, C Loiola 10. **T** 943-428123. *Map 2, F4, p250* Two good places to stay near the new cathedral. They are run by the same family, who can also find rooms in private houses, if these are full.

Ondarreta

AL Hotel Ezeiza, Av Satrustegui 13, **T** 943-214311, **F** 943-214768, www.hotelezeiza.com. *Map 1, C1, p248* Nicely situated at the peaceful western end of Ondarreta beach, this is a welcoming place with the added attraction of an excellent terrace bar. Some of the rooms have great views out over the bay. There's parking available for €7.

AL Hotel La Galeria, C Infanta Cristina 3, **T** 943-216077,
F 943-211298, www.hotellagaleria.com. *Map 1, D1, p248*
Old-fashioned plushness is the order of the day in this imposing
sandstone hotel, guarded by a sphinx. Well located on a quiet
street by the beach, this is better priced than it looks. The rooms
are very elegant and each is themed after a famous painter.

AL Hotel Monte Igueldo, Paseo del Faro 134, **T** 943-210211,
F 943-215028, www.monteigueldo.com. *Map 1, B1, p248* Perched
on Monte Igueldo, this hotel is all about location. Most of the rooms
offer a spectacular view, but it's hardly a peaceful retreat, as the hotel
shares the summit with a tacky amusement park.

F La Sirena, Paseo de Igueldo 25, **T** 943-310268, **F** 943-214090.
Map 1, D1, p248 San Sebastián's HI hostel is close to Ondarreta
beach and easily accessible by bus 24 from town. Curfews, early
check-outs and school groups are the drawbacks but the facilities
are good and both internet access and breakfast are included.

Camping Igueldo, Paseo Padre Orkolaga 69, **T** 943-214502,
F 280411. Open all year, this big San Sebastián campsite is set back
from Ondarreta beach, behind Monte Igueldo.

Gros

LL Villa Soro, Av de Ategorrieta 61, **T** 943-297970, **F** 943-297971,
www.villasoro.com. This hotel is something of an oasis, set in the
large grounds of a sumptuous 19th-century villa with manicured
gardens to the east of Gros. It really feels like a rural hotel, with
discreet service, a refined, relaxing feel and seriously comfortable
rooms, some in an annexe. There's no restaurant, though.

C Pensión Aida, C Iztueta 9, **T** 943-327800, **F** 943-26707,
www.pensionesconencanto.com. *Map 2, C7, p250* This is a good

base that's convenient for the station. The gleaming rooms are appealing and breakfast in bed is a great way to start the day as you mean to continue.

C Pensión Kursaal, C Peña y Goñi 2, **T** 943-292666, **F** 943-297536, www.pensionesconencanto.com. *Map 2, B6, p250* A pleasant place to stay and very near the beach. The attractive rooms have big windows, bathrooms and TV but, as in many of these old buildings, the plumbing and heating can make a racket. There's internet access in the lobby and parking under the Kursaal for €9 a day.

Around San Sebastián

Hondarribia

L Parador de Hondarribia, Pl de Armas 14, **T** 943-645500, **F** 943-642153, www.parador.es. Originally constructed in the 10th century, then reinforced by Carlos V to resist French attacks, the fortified façade shelters a hotel of considerable comfort and delicacy. Rooms don't reach the ornate standard set by the public areas, which bristle with reminders of the building's military function A pretty courtyard and terrace are the highlights.

AL Hotel Obispo, Pl del Obispo s/n, **T** 943-645400, **F** 943-642386, www.hotelobispo.com. The old archbishop's palace is a charming place to stay. a beautiful building, with views across the Bidasoa. The rooms are well-equipped, although they don't quite live up to the gorgeous exterior.

C Iketxe, Barrio Arkoll, near Hondarribia, **T** 943-644391. One of several *agroturismos* around Hondarribia, this very pretty farmhouse is southwest of town, off the road to Irún and past the chapel of Santiagotxo. It's very good value.

D Hostal Alvarez Quintero, C Bernat Etxepare 2, Hondarribia, **T** 943-642299. A tranquil little place with a distinctly old-fashioned air. The rooms are simple and reasonably priced compared to the other options in town but it is a little difficult to find: the entrance is through an arch, on the roundabout by the tourist office.

D Hostal Txoko-Goxoa, C Murrua 22, Hondarribia, **T** 943-644658. A pretty little place on a peaceful, sunny street by the town walls. The rooms are smallish but homely, with flower-filled window boxes.

Oñati and Arantzazu

The cheaper beds in Oñati are booked out quickly at weekends.

D Goiko Venta, Arantzazu 12, **T** 943-781305, **F** 943-780321. On the hill above the monastery, this offers good value, with pleasant rooms, some with a great view of the valley. There's also a restaurant serving hearty roasts and the like.

D Ongi Etorri, C Zaharra 19, Oñati, **T** 943-718285, **F** 943-718284. A family-run, nicely decorated hotel on the main pedestrian street. Rooms have heating and air-conditioning; internet access available.

E Arregi, Ctra Garagaltza-Auzoa 21, **T** 943-780824. An excellent *agroturismo*, a couple of kilometres from Oñati. The big farmhouse is in a green valley with beautiful dark-wood rooms, a ping-pong table and lovely people running it. Meals on request (€10).

E Hospedería de Arantzazu, Arantzazu 29, **T** 943-781313, **F** 943-781314. Right next to the basilica and run by monks, this offers simple but fully equipped rooms in a peaceful atmosphere.

F Echeverria, C Barria 15, Oñati, **T** 943-780460. A cheap *pensión* not far from the main square. Its clean rooms are good value but it's definitely worth ringing ahead at weekends.

Elorrio

There are three *agroturismos* in the countryside around Elorrio, all set in typically solid and attractive Basque farmhouses. **Berriolope**, in the hamlet of Berrio (**T** 946-820640) is the most luxurious, with six attractive doubles in a vine-covered stone building. **Arabio Azpikoa** (Barrio Arabio 8, **T** 946-583342) has simpler but very pleasant rooms, with shared bathrooms, while **Galartxa Barrena** (Zenita, **T** 946-582707) is the closest to Elorrio, and has rooms with or without bath.

A Hotel Elorrio, Bº San Agustín s/n, Elorrio, **T** 946 231555, **F** 946-231663. A short walk from the centre on the Durango road, this modern hotel is not the prettiest but has some good views around the valley and a decent restaurant. It's primarily for business, so it's cheaper at the weekend. The rooms are attractive, airy and light.

F Pensión Nerea, C Pio X 32, Elorrio, **T** 946-820486. A budget-traveller's dream: adequate rooms with shared bathrooms for a pittance. If no-one's about, go to the *tintorería* at Calle Labakua 8.

Vitoria/Gasteiz

L Hotel Canciller Ayala, C Ramón y Cajal 5, **T** 945-130000, **F** 945-133505. Located on Parque de la Florida, this four-star hotel has a lovely setting and excellent facilities but the service lets the whole package down; you get the feeling that if you're not there for a convention, you're nobody.

L Hotel Ciudad de Vitoria, Portal de Castilla 8, **T** 945-141100, **F** 945-143616, www.hoteles-silken.com. Massive four-star hotel on the edge of central Vitoria, where character starts to make way for 'lifestyle'. It's airy and pleasant, with good facilities, including a gym and sauna. The major draw is the incredible weekend rates, with doubles from €67, less than half the weekday rate.

A Hotel Almoneda, C Florida 7, **T** 945-154084, **F** 945-154686, www.hotelalmoneda.com. Attractively situated a few paces from the lovely Parque de la Florida, this hotel has reasonable rooms with a rustic touch – much nicer than the stuffy lobby suggests. Rates are significantly cheaper at weekends. Breakfast included.

C Hotel Páramo, C General Alava 11, **T** 945-140240, **F** 945-140492, www.hotelparamo.com. Strangely located in a shopping arcade, this hotel has snug rooms, with simple but attractive furniture. Plenty of facilities and breakfast included.

C-D Hotel Amarica, C Florida 11, **T** 945-130506. Close to the train station, this friendly hotel is very well placed. The rooms are good value, with TV and a good bathroom. They're also warm and surprisingly quiet, considering it's a busy street.

D Hotel Dato, C Eduardo Dato 28, **T** 945-147230, **F** 945-232320, www.hoteldato.com. This *pintxo*-zone hotel is a treasure-trove of art nouveau and *clásico* statues, mirrors and general plushness. It's comfortable rather than stuffy and the rooms are exceptional value; some have balconies or *miradores*. Recommended.

D Hotel Desiderio, C Colegio San Prudencio 2, **T** 945-251700, **F** 251722. Welcoming cheap hotel with comfy rooms and private bathrooms, on the edge of the Casco Medieval.

D/E Pensión Araba II, C Florida 25, **T** 945-232588. A good base in central Vitoria. There's a variety of clean and comfortable rooms, with or without bathroom, and a genuinely friendly welcome. Parking spaces are available (€6).

F **Casa 400**, C Florida 46, T 945-233887. At this price don't expect many facilities but still, this is clean, comfortable and cheerfully run.

Alava/Araba Province

A **Parador de Argómaniz**, Ctra N1 Km 363, 12 km east of Vitoria, T 945-293200, F 945-293287, www.parador.es. The hamlet of Argómaniz is dominated by a *parador* set in a Renaissance palace. It's a tranquil setting with good views. Napoleon slept here before the disastrous battle of Vitoria. The older part of the building is lovely and contains the restaurant (a beautiful area under the wooden roof) and bar. The rooms, in a more recent annexe, don't reach the same standard but are reasonable value and have all mod cons. A taxi to/from Vitoria costs about €15.

D **Guzurtegi**, Barrio La Plazuela s/n, near Orduña, T 945-399438. A very pretty, hospitable farmhouse, offering full and half board in attractive and comfortable rooms.

D **Merino**, Pl de San Juan 3, Salvatierra, T 945-300052. This bar/restaurant on the main plaza is the best eating option in town. Above it are nice, if slightly overpriced, rooms, with bathroom and TV. It is advisable to book ahead.

D/E **Mendiaxpe**, Barrio Salsamendi 22, near Araia, T 945-304212. Located in the foothills of the Sierra de Urkilla, this *casa rural* is a superb base for walking and has kitchen facilities for guests' use. There are buses between Araia and Vitoria.

Camping Angosto, Ctra Villanañe-Angosto, near Villanañe, T 947-353271, www.camping-angosto.com. On the edge of the Valderejo National Park, this campsite is quite out of the way but has excellent facilities, including bungalows, a bar/restaurant and a swimming pool. It can get busy with families in the summer.

La Rioja Alavesa

The new Frank Gehry-designed complex at the Marqués de Riscal winery in Elciego, due to open in summer 2006, will include a luxury hotel. Check www.westin.com for details and reservations.

A Castillo El Collado, Paseo El Collado 1, Laguardia, **T** 945-621200, **F** 945-621022, www.euskalnet.net/hotelcollado. Decorated in plush and very comfortable style, this mansion at the north end of the old town is beautiful and welcoming and has a good, reasonably priced restaurant.

A Posada Mayor de Migueloa, C Mayor 20, Laguardia, **T** 945-621175, **F** 945-621022, www.mayordemigueloa.com. A beautifully decorated Spanish country house, with a peaceful atmosphere. Rooms have lovely old wooden furniture, plus modern heating and air-conditioning. The restaurant is of a similarly high standard.

B Hotel Antigua Bodega de Don Cosme Palacio, Ctra Elciego s/n, Laguardia, **T** 945-621195, **F** 945-600210, antiguabodega @cosmepalacio.com. A wine-lover's delight. The *bodega* of the old *palacio* has been converted into a charming hotel and restaurant. The sunny rooms are named after grape varietals and come with a free half-bottle. Air-conditioned to cope with the summer heat, most rooms have views over the vines and mountains. Reasonable rates, but some readers have complained of poor service.

D Larretxori, Portal de Páganos s/n, Laguardia, **T/F** 945-600763, larretxori@euskalnet.net. This comfortable *agroturismo* is just outside the city walls and has excellent views over the area. The rooms are spruce and good value and the owner is very benevolent.

Eating and drinking

Eating is one of the things the Basques do best. Most of Spain grudgingly concedes that Basque cuisine is the peninsula's best: the San Sebastián twilight shimmers with Michelin stars, and chummy all-male *txokos* gather in private to swap recipes and cook up feasts in members-only kitchens (see p167). But what strikes the visitor first are the *pintxos* (see p153), a stunning range of bar-top snacks that in many cases seem too pretty to put in your mouth. Basque cuisine is based on seafood, with the Spanish staple *merluza* (hake) featuring alongside *bacalao* (dried salt cod). The latter is definitely an acquired taste but can be delicious. Ingredients used to spice these and other seafoods and meats are typically garlic, peppers and olive oil.

Eating hours are later than most of Europe, although not as late as in other parts of Spain. Lunch is normally served between 1330 and 1500, while, in the evening, most people won't eat until 2130 or 2200 (or later at weekends).

Most restaurants offer a *menú del día*, a three-course meal with wine; this is usually unremarkable but excellent value, costing between €5 and €10. A handful of places offer a similar *menú* in the evening, too. At about 1900 or 2000, while northern Europe is halfway through dinner, Basques are on the streets, strolling up and down the *pasco*, ducking into bars for a swift drink and a *pintxo*, or sitting on a *terraza* somewhere nursing a coffee or a vermouth. Most restaurants don't open in the evening until 2030. On week nights they shut down fairly early (by Spanish standards) but at weekends the *pintxo* bars and restaurants keep buzzing well into the *madrugada*.

Bilbao/Bilbo

Bilbao's Casco Viejo is undoubtedly the place to head for *pintxos* and evening drinking, the best areas being the Plaza Nueva and around the Siete Calles. There's another concentration of bars on Avenida Licenciado Poza and the adjoining Calle García Rivero, while narrow Calle Ledesma, a street back from Gran Vía, is a popular place to head for after-work snacks and drinks. There are some good restaurants in the Casco Viejo (including a couple geared solely to tourists) but also plenty of options scattered through the New Town and Deusto.

Casco Viejo
Metro: Casco Viejo, Tram: Arriaga or Ribera.

€€€ Victor, Pl Nueva 2, **T** 944-151678. *Map 5, D2, p256*
A quality upstairs restaurant with an elegant but relaxed
atmosphere. This is a top place to try Bilbao's signature dish,
bacalao al pil-pil, and there's an excellent wine selection.
Conforms to the general Iberian rule of decreasing vegetables
with increasing price! Recommended.

€€€ Victor Montes, Pl Nueva 8, **T** 944-155603. *Map 5, C3, p256*
This traditional and excellent restaurant is known for its huge
collection of wines and whiskies. The elegant upstairs dining room
has the best of Basque cuisine at surprisingly reasonable prices.
Downstairs is a very popular *pintxo* bar; if you can shoulder your
way to it in the evening, you'll find that not a square inch is free of
posh and delicious bites.

€€ Berton, C Jardines 11, **T** 944-167035. *Map 5, E2, p256*
The hanging *jamones* and bunches of grapes define this cheerful
bar, which has top-notch hammy *pintxos* and *raciones* and some
quality wines by the glass. Packed at weekends and deservedly so.

€€ Egiluz, C Perro 4, **T** 944-150242. *Map 5, E2, p256* Among all
the bright modern lights of the Casco Viejo's newer restaurants,
this sturdy old family-run place is still the place to go if you fancy a
steak or similar. The dining room is upstairs at the back of the bar.
They serve a huge *chuletón* – it could comfortably feed two – and
other excellent grilled and roasted fare.

€€ Kasko, C Santa María, **T** 944-160311. *Map 5, E2, p256* This
busy bar/restaurant has fish- inspired funky decor and high-class
new Basque food. It has a good evening *menú* for €18.50 (€26.50
at weekends) and, sometimes, a pianist entertains diners.

▶ Pintxos

Wherever you go in the Basque country, you'll be confronted and tempted by a massive array of food spread across the top of bars. Many bars serve up very traditional fare: slices of *tortilla* (potato omelette) or *pulgas de jamón* (small rolls with cured ham). Other bars, enthused by 'new Basque' cuisine, take things further and dedicate large parts of their day to creating miniature food sculptures using more esoteric ingredients. The key factor is that they're all meant to be eaten. You can ask the bartender or simply help yourself to what you fancy, making sure to remember what you've had for the final reckoning. If you can't tell what something is, ask (*¿de qué es?*). *Pintxos* usually cost about €1 to €1.20 depending on the bar.

€€ **Pulpería**, C Nueva 4. *Map 5, E1, p256* This recently opened restaurant keeps things attractively simple. Although the setting is elegant and comfortable, the good-value dishes, from Galicia in northwest Spain, are as they should be: hearty *lacón con grelos* stew and tasty octopus (*pulpo*). There's also *paella* (€13.50 per person, order in advance).

€€ **Xukela**, C Perro 2, **T** 944-159772. *Map 5, E2, p256* A very social bar on a very social street. Attractive *pintxos*, a very warm ambience, some good sit-down food – cheeses and cured meats - and a clientele upending glasses of Rioja at competitive pace until comparatively late.

€ **Bar Irintzí**, C Santa María 8. *Map 5, E1, p256* *Pintxos* are an art form in this excellent bar; there´s a superb array of imaginative snacks, carefully labelled, freshly made and compassionately priced. Although a recent refit has removed some of the atmosphere, the taste is as good as ever.

€ **Café-Bar Bilbao**, Pl Nueva 6, **T** 944-151671. *Map 5, D3, p256*
A sparky place with top service and a selection of some of the better gourmet *pintxos* (all labelled) to be had around the old town. It's always busy but the barstaff never seem to miss a trick.

€ **Gatz**, C Santa María 10, **T** 944-154861. *Map 5, E1, p256*
A convivial bar with warm, non-designer decor, friendly people and some of the zone's better *pintxos*. The happy crowd spills onto the street at weekends.

€ **Jaunak**, C Somera 10, **T** 944-159979. *Map 5, E4, p256* One of a few friendly Basque bars on this street, with a range of *bocadillos* and a strong leftist/nationalist vibe.

€ **Laga**, C Merced 2. *Map 5, E2, p256* This bright, simply decorated bar is one of the Casco's best places for no-nonsense wholesome Basque food. Particularly recommended are the croquettes but it's all good, including the fresh fish. Great value.

€ **Río Oja**, C Perro 4, **T** 944-150871. *Map 5, E2, p256* Another good option on this street, specializing in bubbling Riojan stews and Basque fish dishes, most served in big casseroles at the bar. Hearty fare such as *callos* (tripe) or *mollejas*(sweetbreads) banish any chills. It's good value and has friendly service; be aware that the dishes will come microwave-heated, standard practice in Spain.

€ **Rotterdam**, C Perro 6, **T** 944-162165. *Map 5, E2, p256*
Uncomplicated restaurant with a *simpático* boss. This is what lunch restaurants have always been like here, with paper tablecloths and a very solid *menú del día* for €8.50.

€ **Saibigain**, C Barrenkale Barrena 16, **T** 944-150123. *Closed Sun. Map 5, E2, p256* This is an intensely traditional, atmospheric place and one of the best cheap restaurants in the Casco Viejo. It's full of black and white photos of Athletic Bilbao and has a phalanx of hams hanging over the bar. There's a *menú del día* for €8.30. It's worth waiting to grab a table upstairs.

Riverbank

€€€ Guggenheim, Av Abandoibarra 2, **T** 944-239333, www.restauranteguggenheim.com. *Metro: Moyúa, Tram: Guggenheim. Map 4, B6, p254* A good all-round option in the museum. The restaurant is administered by one of San Sebastián's top chefs, and has the quality and prices to match but also offers a *menú del día* for €14 (€18.20 at weekends), which is first rate. No bookings are taken for the *menú*, which is served (slowly) from 1330 on a first-come, first-served basis. The furniture is Gehry's work. Both cafés do a fine line in croissants, coffee and *pintxos*; the one inside, off Gallery 104 has more seating and a nice view over the river.

€ Café Boulevard, C Arenal 3, **T** 944-153128. *Metro: Casco Viejo, Tram: Arriaga. Map 4, C12, p255* Fans of art deco will not want to miss this refurbished defender of the style, founded in 1871 and unchanged since the early 20th century, when it was Bilbao's beloved 'meeting place'. There are plenty of seats, good breakfasts, coffees, *pintxos* and weekday lunchtime *platos combinados*.

€ El Kiosko del Arenal, Muelle del Arenal s/n. *Metro: Casco Viejo, Tram: Arriaga. Map 4, C12, p255* Elegant, cool café under the bandstand in the Arenal. It serves more-than-decent coffee and has plenty of outdoor tables overlooking the river.

El Ensanche

€€€ Bermeo, C Ercilla 37, **T** 944-705700. *Metro: Indautxu. Map 4, G7, p255* Although it's the restaurant of the *Hotel Ercilla*, this deserves its own listing as one of the best places to dine in

Bilbao. Specializing in seafood, which is done both in typical Basque styles and in some innovative modern ways.

€€€ **Guria**, Gran Vía 66, **T** 944-415780. *Metro: San Mamés, Tram: Euskalduna. Map 4, F5, p254* One of Bilbao's top restaurants, with plush red walls lined with watercolours, and a quiet, elegant atmosphere. Its stock-in-trade, like many of its counterparts, is *bacalao*, but prepare to be amazed, as this *bacalao* is a far cry from all those bad renditions produced in other kitchens and factories around the world. There's a *menú de degustación* for €62 and a *menú del día* for €41. Other than these, count on €60 a head minimum, more if you forsake the fish for the meat, which is tender and toothsome. A cheaper option is to eat in the bar, where there's a bistro menu and a very respectable selection of brandies.

€€ **Asador Jauna**, C Juan Zunzunegui 7, **T** 944-417381. *Metro/Tram: San Mamés. Map 3, G2, p252* Despite its characterless location, this is a good choice for the carnivore. The menu is a lot fuller than at other *asadores*, with plenty of fish, as well as venison, duck and other departures from the sirloin and T-bone hierarchy. It's fairly pricey but has a good atmosphere when busy and usually offers a daytime *menú* for around €14.

€€ **Hostaria Marchese del Porto**, C Marqués del Puerto 10, **T** 944-161680. *Metro: Moyúa. Map 4, E9, p255* This elegant Italian restaurant goes slightly over the top with its decor but is deservedly popular with local businessfolk at lunchtime, when an excellent €10 *menú del día* is served in its downstairs *comedor*. Good pasta and *gelati*, too.

€€ **La Viña**, C Henao 27, **T** 944-243602. *Metro: Moyúa. Map 4, D7, p255* You could easily miss this tiny bar wedged into a block in the Ensanche. As well as being a hospitable place to have a glass of wine, it serves some very fine food at a very fair price. The

★ Places to eat *pintxos*

Best

- Bar Irintzi, Bilbao, p153.
- Bar Garriti, San Sebastián, p169.
- La Cuchara de San Telmo, San Sebastián, p170.
- Garbola, San Sebastián, p172.
- Saburdi, Vitoria, p177.

speciality is seafood; you can eat mussels, crab, or whatever's fresh, at the handful of small tables.

€€ Ogetamairu, C Bailén 33, **T** 944-157135, www.ogetamairu.com.
Metro: Abando, Tram: Casino. Map 4, F12, p255 Although not in the greatest of locations, this minimalist two-floor restaurant has won itself a big reputation recently. The clean white dining room hosts an innovative *cocina moderna* that doesn't skimp on quantity. Prices (most mains €12-19) are more than reasonable. You may prefer the more intimate downstairs *comedor*.

€€ Primera Instancia, Alameda Mazarredo 6, **T** 944-236545.
Metro: Abando. Map 4, C10, p255 A buzzy modern bar that's upmarket but far from pretentious. The small restaurant serves a €19.90 *menú de degustación* and a €9 *menú del día*. Check out the snazzy machine that wraps up soggy umbrellas.

€€ Serantes and **Serantes II**, C Licenciado Poza 16, Alameda Urquijo 51, **T** 944-102066. *Metro: Indautxu. Map 4, F8, p255* These two *marisquerías* are not as pricey as their high reputation would suggest, with fish dishes around the €18 mark. The food is very fresh and the chefs have the confidence to let the flavours of the sea hold their own. Go for the daily special, which is usually excellent, or tackle some *cigalas* (Norway lobster), the four-wheel-drive of the prawn world, complete with pincers .

€€ **Su@**, C Marqués del Puerto 4, **T** 944-232292. *Metro: Moyúa. Map 4, D8, p255* One of the latest designer restaurants to open in Bilbao, this is ultra-modern but comfortable, with romantic coloured lighting and a menu of new-style creations that are curiously ordered according to their serving temperature. A gimmick, yes, but the food and atmosphere are pretty good. There's a *menú del día* for €14. Evening bookings essential.

€ **Artajo**, C Ledesma 7, **T** 944-248596. *Metro: Abando, Tram: Casino. Map 4, D10, p255* Uncomplicated bar, with homely wooden tables and chairs and good traditional snacks of *tortilla* and *pulgas de jamón*. Famous for its *tigres* (mussels in spicy tomato sauce).

€ **Buda**, C Ayala 1, **T** 944-157136. *Metro: Abando, Tram: Casino. Map 4, D11, p255* Tucked away behind the Corte Inglés is this modern Asian fusion restaurant. Choices are mainly centred around Japanese and Thai cuisines and are done well. There's a good value *menú* for €8.50, day and night, Monday to Thursday.

€ **Café Iruña**, Jardines de Albia s/n, **T** 944-237021. *Metro: Abando, Tram: Casino. Map 4, C10, p255* This noble old establishment on the Jardines de Albia has reached its century in style. The large building is divided into a nicely refurbished café space, with wood panelling in neo-Moorish style, and an earthier old-style bar with traditional tiled advertisements and some good *pintxos*, including lamb kebabs sizzling on the barbie.

€ **Café La Granja**, Pl Circular 3, **T** 944-230813. *Metro: Abando, Tram: Casino. Map 4, C11, p255* Another spacious old Bilbao café, with attractive art nouveau fittings dating from its foundation in 1926. Its high ceilings and long bar are designed to cope with the lively throng that comes in throughout the day. There are plenty of *pintxos* but the simple *menú del día* is a little overpriced at €10.40.

> ### Dishes to make a Basque of you
>
> - **Bacalao al pil-pil** Salt cod in a yellow sauce made from oil, garlic and the natural gelatin of the fish. Originally eaten during the Carlist siege of Bilbao, the sauce is something of a phenomenon, suddenly turning thick and yellow on cooking.
> - **Kokotxas** Fish cheeks. Delicious.
> - **Alubias de Tolosa** The Rolls Royce of beans (see p175) is best served with pickled cabbage and chunks of meat.
> - **Pochas a la Riojana** Another favourite bean dish.
> - **Txangurro relleno** Spider crab blended with fish, tomato, onion and spices and served in its shell. Supreme.
> - **Idiazábal con membrillo** The Basque sheep's milk cheese packs a punch and is superbly offset by the sweet quince jelly.

€ **Café Monaco**, Alameda de Recalde 34, **T** 944-238684. _Metro: Moyúa._ _Map 4, E7, p255_ A good choice for breakfast, with quality coffee and _pintxos_. The host seems to have a soft spot for the Principality of Monaco and Athletic Bilbao.

€ **Capuccino**, C Godórniz 2, **T** 944-436980. _Metro: Indautxu._ _Map 4, G8, p255_ A place to go for people in the know. This café, run by a friendly Egyptian, and with a map of the old Nile painted on the roof, serves great filled pitta rolls, as well as shawarma, musaka, and other snacks. They have an excellent range of teas too.

€ **Don Chufo**, C Iparraguirre 17, **T** 944-235499. _Metro: Moyúa._ _Map 4, D7, p255_ The sleek decor belies a long-standing lunchtime favourite, serving warming traditional food. It's within striking distance of the Guggenheim and has a good €10 lunch _menú._

€ **Fresc Co**, C Ledesma 12, **T** 944 233001. _Metro: Abando, Tram: Guggenheim._ _Map 4, C10, p255._ A brash newcomer on traditional

Calle Ledesma, this vast, brightly lit but comfortable spot is a real sign of the changing times in Spain. It offers, to the astonishment of old-timers, a large vegetarian buffet weekday evenings and all day at weekends for €9.50.

€ **Garibolo**, C Fernández del Campo 7, **T** 944-273255. *Metro: Moyúa. Map 4, G10, p255* At first glance, Bilbao doesn't seem a large enough Spanish city to sustain more than one vegetarian restaurant, but the colourful Garibolo packs 'em in, particularly for its €10 lunch special. A range of Asian-inspired dishes as well as stuffed aubergine (recommended) and organic wines.

€ **La Embajada**, C Iparraguirre 9, **T** 944-245166. *Metro: Moyúa, Tram: Guggenheim. Map 4, D7, p255* A relaxed little café-bar with a terrace that's a great spot for a cold beer and a *pintxo* on a summer's day. The idiosyncratic decor includes a lampshade made from cans and metal hoses; there's a colourful toucan overseeing proceedings.

€ **Lekeitio**, C Diputación 1, **T** 944-239240. *Metro: Moyúa. Map 4, D9, p255* Attentive staff work at this mile-long bar, which has a fantastic selection of after-work eats. There's a good variety of fishy and seafoody *pintxos*, as is the *tortilla*. A palisade of oars and lifebuoys sections off a small sit-down eating area.

€ **Mr Lee**, C Pedro Martínez Artola 12, **T** 944-442328. *Metro: Indautxu. Map 4, H10, p255* Free of the paraphernalia that adorns other Chinese restaurants in Spain and tends to turn them into caricatures of themselves, this has an elegant, spacious dining area, with Asian artwork of restrained good taste. The menu has a range of decent good-value dishes from different parts of east and southeast Asia. The street slopes up from Plaza Zabálburu.

€ **New Inn**, Alameda Urquijo 9, **T** 944-151043. *Metro: Moyúa. Map 4, E10, p255.* The restored art nouveau splendour in the main bar of this popular lunch spot is reason enough to enter. Workers in busy Bilbao offices sadly have little time to grab a three-course meal, so this place offers a range of excellent sandwiches and similar.

€ **Okela**, C García Rivero 8, **T** 944-415937. *Metro: Indautxu. Map 4, G7, p255* One of several smart choices on this busy little street, this is popular with the office crowd and dominated by a huge signed photo of the footballer Joseba Etxebarría (when he had more hair) in full stride for Athletic Bilbao. The *pintxos* are elaborate and excellent.

€ **Taberna Taurina**, C Ledesma 5, **T** 944-241381. *Metro: Abando, Tram: Casino. Map 4, C11, p254* A tiny old-time tiles 'n' sawdust bar that is packed top-to-bottom with bullfighting memorabilia. The old pictures convey something of the sport's noble side. The *tortilla* here also commands respect.

€ **Zuretzat**, C Iparraguirre 7, **T** 944-248505. *Metro: Moyúa, Tram: Guggenheim. Map 4, C6, p254* A decent bar decked out with prints of ships from the golden days of the ocean liner, as well as the hard hats of the workers who built the Guggenheim. Prices reflect passing tourist trade.

€ **Zuripot**, C Licenciado Poza and Av Dr Areilza. *Metro: Indautxu, Tram: Sabino Arana. Map 4, G6, p254* A solid corner choice decorated with clowns and strange ceramic figures. Superb, if skimpy, *tortilla*.

Deusto/Deustu
Metro: Deustu.

€€ **Casa Vasca**, Av Lehendakari Aguirre 13-15, **T** 944-483980. *Map 4, E1, p254* A Deusto institution. The front bar has a good selection of posh *pintxos* and a couple of comfortable nooks to settle into, with a slightly pricey drink. Behind is a restaurant that serves authentic Basque cuisine in generous portions. Another dining room serves a €10 *menú del día* and there's even a nightclub downstairs, catering for a grown-up crowd.

€€ **Oriotarra**, C Blas de Otero 30, **T** 944-470830. *Map 4, E1, p254* A classy *pintxo* bar that has won an award for the best bar snack in Bilbao. A round of applause for the pig's ear *millefeuille*.

€€ **Taloaska**, Av Madariaga 7, **T** 944-758264. *Map 4, E1, p254* A more than solid choice in the heart of Deusto, with a bar that stretches as far as the eye can see and is very well endowed with *pintxos*. At the end is the dining room, where a good *menú* is served for €10.50.

€ **El Café de Deusto**, Av Lehendakari Aguirre 9. *Map 4, E1, p254.* This comfortable, old-style café on Deusto's main street has elegant wood panels, ornate stained-glass lampshades and painted depcitions of old life in the Republic. It's especially loved for its selection of *tortilla* with various delicious fillings.

€ **Txoko del Vino**, C Blas de Otero 26, **T** 944-763564. *Map 4, E1, p254* A bar that couldn't be less glamorous or more authentic, with cheap wine and hams that might have been cured by the cigar smoke. Great traditional atmosphere.

Getxo and around

€€€ **Jolastoki**, Av Leioa 24, **T** 944-912031. *Metro: Neguri.* Decorated in classy but homely country mansion style, Jolastoki is a house of good repute throughout Euskadi. The traditional dishes here, such as *caracoles en salsa vizcaína* (snails in Vizcayan sauce) and *liebre* (hare), are the sort of treats that give Basque cuisine its lofty reputation.

€€€ **Kukai (Kubita Kaia)**, Muelle de Arriluze 10-11,
T 944-600103. *Metro: Neguri.* A highly acclaimed restaurant with
views over the water from Getxo's marina. People swear by the
cigalas (Norway lobsters) turned out by young modern chef Alvaro
Martínez. Not to be confused with another restaurant named
Cubita, which is next to the windmill above Arrigunaga beach.

€€ **Asador Goietz**, C Aretxondo 14, **T** 944-603883. *Metro:
Algorta.* Located in the old port area, this restaurant specializes in
grilling fish over open coals. It also has several varieties of crab on
offer to test your taste buds.

€€ **Karola Etxea**, C Aretxondo 22, **T** 944-600868. *Metro:
Algorta.* Perfectly situated in a quiet lane above the old port, this is
a good place to try some fish; there are usually a few varieties
available, such as *txitxarro* (scad) or *besugo* (sea bream). The
kokotxas (cheeks and throats of hake in sauce) are also delicious.

€ **El Hule**, C Victor Chavarri 13, **T** 944-722104. *Euskotren:
Portugalete.* In the narrow, sloping streets of Portugalete's old
town (just behind the town hall near the Puente Colgante), this is a
cracking spot for lunch. The cute little upstairs and downstairs
dining rooms are cosy and comfortable and the food is
high-quality, traditional, uncomplicated fare (*menú del día* €9.50),
served with a smile.

€ **Irrintzi**, C Particular de Arlamendi, off C Zalama, **T** 944-643372.
Metro: Areeta. This homely bar has appealing brick-and-wood
decor, an upmarket clientele and about the finest reputation for
pintxos on the right bank of the *ría*. There's an excellent array and
they are all very tempting. From Areeta Metro, go straight ahead
and uphill, past the Mandarin Chinese restaurant, then turn right.
The bar is not marked.

€ Zodiako's, C Euskal Herria s/n (corner of Telletxe),
T 944-604059. *Metro: Algorta.* This bar in the heart of Getxo is one
of the area's best, with a terrace, *pintxos* and friendly service.
Underneath is Alai, a weekend *discoteca*.

Basque coastline

Bermeo and Mundaka

€€ Asador Bodegón, Kepa Deuna 1, Mundaka, **T** 946-876353.
This is Mundaka's best restaurant, despite its slight air of 'we know
what the tourists want'. Meat and, especially, fresh fish are grilled
to perfection over the coals. Try the home-made *patxarán*, a
liqueur made from sloe berries. Upstairs is Casino, a traditional
members' club that's also a high-quality restaurant, with a very
old-fashioned feel and great views from the gallery.

€ Batzokia, main square, Mundaka. The €9.90 *menú del día* can
be a good opportunity to try the local catch at a discount.

€ Ereperi, San Pelaio s/n, between Bakio and Bermeo,
T 946-194065. A good restaurant overlooking San Juan de
Gaztelagutxe, with a superb terrace and a cheap lunch *menú*.

Gernika and around

€€ Lezika, Cuevas de Santamamiñe, Kortezubi, **T** 946-252975.
The whole of Vizcaya seems to descend on the beer garden here at
weekends, with kids and dogs in tow. The restaurant is better value
than the meagre *raciones* on offer at the bar.

€ Gernika, C Industria 2, **T** 946-250778. One of several choices on
Gernika's main eating street, this is an appealing spot for lunch as

well as a sociable bar. There's a *menú* for €9.50, which usually includes a good lentil or bean stew. This, plus the friendly, bustling service ensures that everyone leaves contented.

Lekeitio

€€€ Oxangoiti Jauregia, C Gamarra 2, **T** 946-843151. An upmarket restaurant in a historic building next to the town hall. There's a smart wooden interior, a craft shop and tasty seafood at fairly stiff prices.

€€ Emperatriz Zita, Santa Elena Etorbidea s/n, **T** 946-842655. The restaurant in this seafront hotel is well priced

€€ Hotel Beitia, Av Pascual Abaroa 25, **T** 946-840111. The restaurant is a much better bet than the hotel, with high-quality seafood and a pleasant patio.

€€ Kaia, Txatxo kaia 5, **T** 946-840284. One of many harbourside restaurants, this serves fairly upmarket, tasty fish.

€€ Restaurante Zapirain, Igualdegui 5, **T** 946-840255. A fish restaurant which is popular with Lekeitians as well as visitors. It's traditional in style and welcoming in manner.

Ondarroa

€€ Eretegia Joxe Manuel, C Sabino Arana 23, **T** 946-830104. Although it does a range of other appetizing dishes, this restaurant is best known for its outdoor charcoal grill, which caters for carnivores with large appetites. Forget quarter-pounders; here the steaks approach the kilogram mark and are very tasty. About €30 a head. Recommended.

€ Sutargi, Nasa Kalea 11, **T** 946-832258. A popular bar with a good-value restaurant upstairs: main dishes are €9-14.

Getaria and around

€€€ Kaia, C Katrapona Aundia 10, **T** 943-140500. The best and priciest of Getaria's restaurants has a sweeping view over the harbour and a high standard of food and service. Whole fish, grilled over the coals outside, is a highlight, as is the exceptional and reasonable wine list. Try some of the local *txakolí*; it's the best around.

€€ Asador Mayflower, C Katrapona 4, **T** 943-140658. One of a number of *asadores* in this attractive harbour town, with an excellent *menú del día*. Grilled sardines are a tasty speciality.

€€ Kulixka, C Bixkonde 1, Zarautz, **T** 943-831300. Welcoming waterfront restaurant with an unbeatable view of the beach. Good seafood, as you'd expect, and a decent *menú del día* for €10, as well as an evening menu for €15 and a €25 special. There are several other good eateries in town.

€ Politena, Kale Nagusia 9, **T** 943-140113. A bar orientated towards weekend visitors from Bilbao and San Sebastián. It serves a very enticing selection of *pintxos* and a €12.50 weekend *menú*, which isn't bad either.

€ Txalupa, C Herrerieta 1, **T** 943-140592. A hospitable bar that's a great place to buy or taste the local fish and *txakolí*. There are *pintxos* on offer, as well as *cazuelitas*, small portions of bubbling stews or seafood in sauce.

San Sebastián/Donostia

Eating is an important part of life throughout the Basque country but San Sebastián is the undisputed food capital, perhaps because local people have more time and cash on their hands. Several of the best restaurants in the business are to be found here, and modern Guipúzcoan chefs make waves worldwide.

The most unusual aspect of San Sebastián's culinary scene is the existence of *txokos*, or gastronomic societies, which have made the city their spiritual home. Most are private clubs with an all-male membership. The three key elements of a *txoko* are a members' lounge, a dining room and a vast kitchen. The members gather to swap recipes and prepare massive gourmet meals to be devoured by themselves, friends and family. It's invitation only so if you want to experience a *txoko*, your best bet is to look around San Sebastián and make friends with a tubby man who has a twinkle in his eye. Alternatively, contact **Epiculinary** (T 1-847 295 5363, 1-888 380 9010 toll free in the US, www.epiculinary.com), which organizes all-inclusive tours, gourmet meals and cooking lessons from society members.

The best places for *pintxos* are in the Parte Vieja, which teems with bars. Gros is a quieter option. Restaurants abound in the old town too, particularly on Calle Fermín Calbetón, which has several excellent places. Some of the best are further afield, however, in the new town or outside the city limits. *Sagardotegiak* (cider houses) speckle the hills south of town (see p96).

Parte Vieja

€€€ **Casa Nicolasa**, C Aldamar 4, **T** 943-421762. *Map 2, B5, p250* This simple and gracious second-floor dining room is the setting for one of the city's best restaurants. The emphasis is on seafood – the *almejas* (small clams) with trout roe are superb – and the service is restrained and attentive.

€€€ **Panier Fleuri**, Paseo Salamanca 2, **T** 943-424205. *Map 2, B5, p250* An airy split-level restaurant with a French-inspired menu and an emphasis on fresh market produce and charcoal-grilled meats.

€€€ **Urepel**, Paseo Salamanca 3, **T** 943-424040. *Map 2, B5, p250* A long, brooding restaurant with a Spanish feel. The food is lighter than the decor might suggest. The highlight is an elegant shellfish dish. A good wine list accompanies the classy nosh.

€€ **Barbarin**, C Puerto 21, **T** 943-421886. *Map 2, B3, p250* A friendly, comfortable, well-priced restaurant that's spacious and wood-beamed. It specializes in local seafood. The *rollitos de txangurro* (fried crab rolls) are especially tempting but the paella and the cheap steaks are good, too.

€€ **Bodegón Alejandro**, C Fermín Calbetón 4, **T** 943-427158. *Map 2, B4, p250* This popular spot is overseen by celebrated chef Martín Berasategui and has become very popular. With a homely, unpretentious interior, the emphasis is on the quality cuisine, which is French in focus. There's a daily *menú* for €11.50 and an excellent bistro menu in the evenings for €29.50. Curt service is the only downside.

€€ **Casa Gandarias**, C 31 de Agosto 25, **T** 943-428106. *Map 2, B3, p250* This busy bar near the Santa María church has an adjoining restaurant but its *pintxos* are excellent and are served by efficient and cordial staff. The *solomillo* and the grilled *foie* are particularly recommended. Good whisky selection.

€€ **Casa Urola**, C Fermín Calbetón 20, **T** 943-423424. *Map 2, B4, p250* An enticing choice, whether for *pintxos* or a full meal, this small and busy bar has exquisite gourmet snacks on the counter. There are two dining areas; upstairs is more peaceful. There are excellent fish dishes and tasty *solomillo*. Recommended.

€€ **Ganbara**, C San Jerónimo 21, **T** 943-422575. *Map 2, B3, p250* This is a fairly upmarket bar and *asador*, with a worthwhile array of *pintxos* to accompany the cheerfully poured wine. The *raciones* are delicious, with such delicacies as *trufas* (truffles) and *percebes* (goose barnacles) making an appearance.

€€ **Munto**, C Fermín Calbetón 17, **T** 943-426088. *Map 2, B4, p250* This thoroughly enjoyable place is one of many good choices on this street. The downstairs *comedor* is attractively lit and decorated, the service is attentive and the food – tasty steaks and delicately treated seafood – is of excellent quality for the price.

€ **Barandiaran**, Alameda del Boulevard 28, **T** 943-429796. *Map 2, C3, p250* Despite its location, this is a very authentic café with a loyal following, who come for strong coffee and tumblers of wine.

€ **Bar Garriti**, C San Juan 8. *Map 2, B4, p250* An unglamorous bar by the La Bretxa centre that's been going for years. Somewhat surprisingly, on entering you are confronted with a mightily impressive spread of *pintxos*. You could spend all day in here if you weren't careful.

€ **Casa Vergara**, C Mayor 21, **T** 943 431073. *Map 2, B3, p250* This highly recommended bar is on the corner of the ever-popular 31 de Agosto. While it's worth sitting down in the simple but comfortable *comedor* to try *raciones* of stews – *callos* (tripe), *chipirones* (squid) or *pulpo* (octopus) – the *pintxos* and the service at the bar are delightful. Try the *gulas* wrapped in smoked salmon, if they're available. It's well priced, too.

€ **La Cepa**, C 31 de Agosto 7, **T** 943-426394. *Map 2, A4, p250* Perenially and deservedly popular bar lined with hams and featuring the head of a particularly large *toro* on the wall. Good atmosphere and *pintxos* and *raciones* to match.

€ **La Cuchara de San Telmo**, C 31 de Agosto 28 (back),
T 943-420840. *Map 2, A4, p250* An extraordinary bar at the side
of the Museo de San Telmo. The kitchen serves made-to-order
gourmet dishes in miniature for €2-2.50. It's original and inspiring.
Recommended.

€ **Portaletas**, C Puerto 8, **T** 943-423888. *Map 2, B3, p250* This
welcoming establishment has stone-faced walls and wooden
beams and offers unpretentious hospitality along with appetizing
pintxos, mostly on slices of bread. There's also a cheap *menú del día*
and good-value *raciones* (€5-10).

€ **Ttun Ttun Taberna**, C San Jerónimo 25, **T** 943-426882. *Map 2,
B3, p250* Amid all the class and sophistication of San Sebastián,
this earthy Basque restaurant is a favourite of fishermen and other
local folk, who need a good solid meal. The authentic and reliable
menú, eaten in a haze of chatter and cigar smoke, costs just €7.50.

Centro and new town

€€ **Altuna Berri**, C San Martín 43, **T** 943-451350. *Map 2, F4,
p250.* This compact bar is run by very decent people and has a
short but excellent *menú* for €11.90, as well as tasty *raciones* – the
eggs are particularly popular. It's an excellent spot for lunch, not
far from the beach.

€€ **Café de la Concha**, Paseo de la Concha s/n, **T** 943-473600.
Map 2, F2, p250 This is a pretty place to stop for a coffee or a glass
of wine during a stroll along the beach. There's also a reasonable
restaurant with fabulous views and a €10 *menú del día*. There's a
great outdoor terrace where you can eat for a €1 supplement.

€€ **Iruaritz**, Av Libertad 40, **T** 943-433332. *Map 2, D4, p250*
This historic café-bar attracts a genteel San Sebastián crowd. It

has a *salón* atmosphere, with regular dancing exhibitions and attractive stained glass behind the bar. The restaurant offers *menús* for €12 and €17.

€€ Oquendo, C Oquendo 8, **T** 943-420932. *Map 2, C5, p250*
A good, fairly formal restaurant near Hotel María Cristina, serving a range of fresh fish for around €18 a plate. There is some good bar-top eating to be had and the photo wall from the San Sebastián Film Festival is great for testing your silver-screen knowledge; the owner makes it into most of the shots.

Ondarreta

€€ Restaurante San Martín, Plazoleta Funicular, **T** 943-214084. *Map 1, C1, p248* Next to the Igueldo funicular, this pretty house on a hill is a restaurant specializing in fish and the odd game bird. There are great views from the dining room and you can also eat outdoors.

Gros

€€€ Kursaal Restaurant, Av Zurriola 1, **T** 943-003162. *Map 2, A6, p250* One of several restaurants overseen by the top local chef Martín Berasategui, this one is attractively set in the Kursaal and features the most modern of Basque *nouvelle cuisine*. Considering the quality on offer, it's not too pricey – you can eat well for €50 a head – and there are various *menús de degustación*. There is also a café, which is an excellent spot for an early evening *pintxo* and a drink, with superb views over the river mouth and the sea.

€ Aloña Berri, C Bermingham 24, **T** 943-290818. *Map 2, A8, p250* It's surprising the staff don't weep when a customer wolfs down a *pintxo* here; so much effort seems to have gone into making them look pretty.

€ **Garbola**, Paseo Colón 11, **T** 943-285019. *Map 2, B7, p250*
Garbola is a local legend in its own *pintxo*-time thanks to its
scrumptious mushroom creations and Caipirinhas. It also offers
more unusual snacks, such as kangaroo and shark. The interior is
very plush and upmarket, and the dapper owner will keep
tempting you with further delights.

Southern hills

€€€ **Zuberoa**, Bº Iturriotz 8, near Oiartzun/Oyarzun, **T** 943-
491228. *Closed Sun night and all day Mon.* This attractive stone
farmhouse, with a wooden porch and terrace, is the lair of top chef
Hilario Arbelaitz and his brothers, whose cooking combines essential
Basqueness with the very best of Mediterranean and French cuisine.
Everything on the menu is delicious, from the typical fish soup to the
sort of thing not even dreamed of elsewhere, such as a grapefruit,
spider crab and trout roe jelly with potato and olive oil cream. For a
real gastronomic experience, order the €96 *menú de degustación*, a
once-in-a-lifetime 11-course symphony of food (drinks extra).

€€ **Sansonategi**, Bº Martindegi s/n, **T** 943-553260. One of the
few cider houses to be open for meals all year, Sansonategi offers a
traditional *menú sidrería* for €24, as well as good à la carte choices.

Around San Sebastián

Hondarribia

€€€ **Sebastián**, C Mayor 9, **T** 944-3640167. Set in a dingy
old grocery packed with interesting aromas, is a restaurant that
some consider to be one of the best in Euskadi. The food certainly
exceeds the humble decor and there's a good value *menú de
degustación* for €38. Tasty *foie*, too.

€€ Medievo, Pl Guipúzcoa 8, **T** 943-644509. Dubious as it sounds, the 21st-century medieval decor works, as does the imaginatively prepared food, such as venison with prunes. There's an €11 *menú del día*; otherwise budget on €30 per head.

€ Bar Itxaropena, C San Pedro 67, **T** 943-641197. Good bar in the New Town offering a variety of cheap foodstuffs and some good company at weekends.

Inland from San Sebastián
All the accommodation options in Arantzazu have restaurants.

€€ Nico, C Gernikako Arbola 4, Elorrio, **T** 946-820469. This first-floor restaurant looks over the heart of the town and serves up wholesome and hearty homestyle food in spacious surroundings.

€ Arkupe, Pl del los Fueros 9, Oñati, **T** 943-781699. A good bar-restaurant on Onati's main square, with a variety of cheap *raciones* and *platos*. It's the focus of the early evening outdoor drinking scene. There's a *menú del día* for €8.50.

€ Izarraitz, C Zaharra 5, Oñati. A very warm and welcoming *pintxo* bar on the pedestrian street. It's the focus of the lively wine-drinking scene at weekends.

€ Parra Taberna, Elorrio. A peaceful café and bar with tables on the main square. The interior features beautiful glass and stone. Internet access available.

Vitoria/Gasteiz

The old town is good for bars, which are nearly all clustered along Calle Cuchillería. The pedestrian Calle Eduardo Dato and the streets crossing it are excellent for the early evening *pintxo* trail.

Casco Medieval

€€€ Arkupe, C Mateo Moraza 13, **T** 945-230080. A quality restaurant serving imaginative dishes, such as a tasty squid and potato pie, and inspiring salads. The *menú de degustación* is €33.

€€ Asador Matxete, Pl Machete 4, **T** 945-131821. A stylish modern restaurant has been harmoniously incorporated into this pretty plaza above Los Arquillos. It specializes in meat, expertly grilled over coals. There's also a pleasant terrace on which to enjoy a drink in this peaceful square.

€€ Zabala, C Mateo Moraza 9, **T** 945-230099. Although you wouldn't know it from the basic decor, this is a very well-regarded local restaurant. Solid rather than spectacular, the dishes include tasty game-based stews, featuring pigeon, hare or partridge. Good salads, chops and steaks round out the menu, and the friendly family service makes it one of Vitoria's most satisfying choices.

€ Bar El 7, C Cuchillería 7, **T** 945-272298. An excellent bar at the head of the Casco Medieval's liveliest street. Its big range of *bocadillos* keeps students and all-comers happy. Order a half if you're not starving, as the portions are pretty large. There's also a very acceptable lunchtime menu for €9.50.

€ Hala Bedi, C Cuchillería 98, **T** 945-260411. A Basque bar with a cheerful atmosphere and late closing at night. Out of a tiny kitchen come *crêpes* with a massive variety of sweet and savoury fillings. Good value and friendly.

€ Parral, Canton de San Francisco Javier 4, **T** 945-276833. This relaxed spot on a sloping street above Calle Cuchillería is a vegetarian restaurant by day and a mood bar by night, with

Bean feast

For many in the English-speaking world the word 'beans' is about as far as it gets from the word 'gourmet'. Instead it conjures up memories of school dinners, tail-between-the-legs pre-payday trips to the supermarket and barely warm breakfasts at a dodgy B&B.

In Spain, however, beans are taken seriously, especially in the Basque lands, and there are more varieties than you'd care to name. In Alava, *pochas* are esteemed: soft, whiteish and picked very young. Vitoria rates *habas* (broadbeans) very highly, while beans *a la Vizcaína* go down a treat in Bilbao. The Brazil of the bean World Cup, however, is Tolosa (near San Sebastián)

Alubias de Tolosa are to Heinz baked beans what caviar is to grit. Small and dark red in colour, they are traditionally cooked in clay pots. Tolosans will tell you that the beans only taste their best when cooked in hard Tolosan water. Tolosan beans have a *Denominación de Origen*, much like wine, and there's an annual contest among the official growers.

Alubias de Tolosa are traditionally eaten with pork, *morcilla* (blood sausage) and cabbage. This is a delicious winter warmer dish if done properly (if not, it can be tasteless) but it can be heavy on the stomach in the sweaty summer heat.

regular live music. There's a salad buffet as well as a good value *menú del día*.

€ **Sherezade**, C Correría 42, **T** 945-255868. A relaxed café that's frequented by students. It serves up good coffee and a range of *infusiones* (herb and fruit teas).

El Ensanche

€€€ Dos Hermanas, C Madre Vedruna 10, **T** 945-132934. One of Vitoria's oldest restaurants is not the place to come for *nouvelle cuisine*. Instead enjoy generous, hearty and delicious traditional dishes. There's a *menú de degustación* for €39.

€€€ Ikea, Portal de Castilla 27, **T** 943-144747. Lovers of Swedish homewares will be disappointed to discover that this is in fact one of Vitoria's best restaurants. It's mainly French in style, with a few traditional Basque dishes. There's a *menú de degustación* for €48, although ordering *à la carte* needn't cost much more. The crunchy squab (*pichón*) in a red wine sauce is memorable.

€€ Baztertxo, Pl de España 14. A fine bar with some great wines by the glass and top-notch *jamón*. Service can be beneath the dignity of the staff but it's a good choice nonetheless.

€€ Izaga, Tomás de Zumárraga 2, **T** 945-138200. Excellent eating is to be had in this fairly formal restaurant in a smart stone building. The focus is seafood but there are plenty of other specialities (mains €13-22) – duck's liver on stuffed pig's ear, for example – and some sinful desserts.

€€ Restaurante Urdiña, C San Antonio 22, **T** 945-233242. Despite the unattractive interior, there's some good nosh served here. The emphasis is on simple traditional dishes done well. There's a *menú del día* for €9 and a *menú de degustación* at a more hefty €22.50.

€€ Xixilu, Pl América 2, **T** 945-230068. On a small garden square not far from the train station, this is a great place to eat. The sociable, intimate *comedor* at the back is filled with chunky wooden tables and stools. The food is quite smart, with a tasty *solomillo con foie* and good house salad among a range of tempting dishes. Recommended.

€ **Café Moderno**, Pl España 4, **T** 945-234448. Sun seekers should head here in the afternoon, when the terrace in the picture-perfect arcaded square is ideally placed for maximum rays.

€ **Cuatro Azules Florida**, Parque de la Florida, **T** 945-148848. One of Vitoria's best spots has lots of tables amid the trees of this peaceful park. Regular games of boules take place nearby.

€ **Restaurante JG**, C Eduardo Dato 27, **T** 945-231132. There are some excellent *pintxo* bars in Vitoria and this is one of them. The range of *croquetas* come highly recommended. More substantial eating is also good value in the *comedor*.

€ **Saburdi**, C Eduardo Dato 32, **T** 945-147016. Another classic option for *pintxos* on this pedestrian street, with a great range of delicious bites. It's warmly lit and welcoming, with several decent wines by the glass. Recommended.

€ **Taberna**, C San Prudencio 21, **T** 945-231004. A simple but winning formula: long bar, tables in the sun, big screen showing sport or films, beer, wine and *pintxos*.

Alava/Araba Province

Salvatierra

€€ **Merino**, Pl de San Juan 3, **T** 945-300052. A sombre but reasonable bar- restaurant; the best option in town.

€ **Jose Mari**, C Mayor 73, **T** 945-300042. This is a solid local café with an attached restaurant doing a decent-value daytime and evening *menú* for €8.50. Smiles can sometimes cost extra, though!

La Rioja Alavesa

€€€ **Mesón La Cueva**, Concepción 15, Oyon, **T** 945-601022. If you're visiting wineries over this way, a hearty lunch here is in order. It's a place with a lofty and deserved reputation, in the heart of the village. The new upstairs *comedor*, which is light and airy, is a bonus. The *menú* costs €20 and features some excellent Riojan staples, such as *pochas* (young broad beans) and other hearty stews. Recommended.

€€ **Castillo El Collado**, Paseo El Collado 1, Laguardia, **T** 945-621200. There's an excellent, well-priced restaurant in this beautiful fortified hotel at the northern end of Laguardia.

€€ **El Bodegón**, Travesía Santa Engracia 3, Laguardia, **T** 945-600793. Tucked away in the middle of old Laguardia is this cosy restaurant, with a €11 *menú del día* focusing on the hearty staples of the region, such as *pochas* or *patatas con chorizo*.

€€ **Hotel Antigua Bodega de Don Cosme Palacio**, Ctra Elciego s/n, Laguardia, **T** 945-621195. *Closed Sun evening and all day Mon.* This hotel restaurant showcases local cuisine, with a couple of challenging *menús*, as well as *à la carte* dishes.

€€ **Marixa**, C Sancho Abarca s/n, Laguardia, **T** 945-600165. The dining room of the the Hotel Marixa is a good place to eat and boasts great views over the vine-covered plains below. A range of local specialities are served by formally correct Spanish waiters. The wine list isn't bad either.

The distinction between different types of hostelry is never clear in Spain. What starts the day as a coffee 'n' croissant stop for office workers might end the night with the lights dimmed, the music pumping and frighteningly large gin and tonics being poured. The listings in this section are generally places that open late, close late and don't serve food. All three cities have plenty of bars; Bilbao inevitably offers more options, although in summer San Sebastián gives it a run for its money. Many are only open at the weekend, however; Basques aren't big midweek revellers. The clubbing scene in the Basque lands isn't great. Bona fide clubs (*discotecas*) are fairly few in number, and many are solely devoted to the Spanish Top Four. San Sebastián has a number of high-profile *discotecas* which complement its beachside scene but more interesting venues are to be found in Bilbao. Many clubs don't open their doors until after midnight and keep things going until well after dawn. Few are open during the week.

Bilbao/Bilbo

Bilbao's nightlife is fairly quiet during the week but it makes up for it at weekends. Nearly everywhere in the Casco Viejo shuts by 0130 but you can always dash across the Puente de la Merced to the streets around Calle Hernani. Be careful in this zone, though, as muggings are not unknown. Most bars have to shut at 0400 these days, but there are some *discotecas* that stay open later.

Bars

Bilbo Rock, Muelle de la Merced s/n, **T** 944-151306. *Metro: Casco Viejo, Tram: Mercado. Map 4, E12, p255* Atmospheric venue in a converted church that's now a temple of live rock. Bands play most nights at 2100 or 2200. No licence but canned beer is available.

Bizitza, C Torre 1. *Metro: Casco Viejo, Tram: Mercado. Map 5, E2, p256* Very chilled, predominantly gay bar with a Basque political slant and frequent cultural events. The staff mix great drinks to ensure that this is one of the best spots for an after-dinner *copa* in Bilbao. Recommended.

Café Lamiak, C Pelota 8, **T** 944-161765. *Metro: Casco Viejo, Tram: Arriaga. Map 5, F2, p256* A relaxed two-floor forum: the sort of place a literary genre, pressure group or world-famous funk band might start out. Mixed crowd.

Cómic's, C Príncipe 3. *Metro: Abando, Tram: Ayuntamiento. Map 4, B11, p255* A cheery, boisterous place with some interesting music and a very late last-drinks call at weekends.

Compañia del Ron, C Máximo Aguirre 23. *Metro: Moyúa. Map 4, F7, p255* Despite the chain pub feel, this is a good early-evening spot, with over 100 rums at the bar staff's disposal.

El Patio de mi Casa, C Cosme Echevarrieta 13. *Metro: Moyúa, Tram: Guggenheim. Map 4, C8, p255* A small but quality place, which serves great *copas* to a discerning crowd in a homely, relaxed atmosphere until 0300 or thereabouts.

Errondabide, C Ronda 20. *Metro: Casco Viejo, Tram: Mercado. Map 5, E4, p256* This is an archetypal pro-independence Basque bar. There are political posters everywhere, photos of ETA prisoners, a spirited atmosphere and plenty of smoke and beer.

K2, C Somera 10. *Metro: Casco Viejo, Tram: Mercado. Map 5, E4, p256* One of the last to shut in the Casco on weeknights, this is a big bar with seating, exhibitions on the walls and a varied crowd.

Luz Gas, C Pelota 6, **T** 944-790823. *Metro: Casco Viejo, Tram: Mercado. Map 5, F2, p256* A beautiful mood bar with an oriental touch. It's sophisticated but friendly and you can challenge all-comers to a game of chess or Connect 4.

Mitote, C Belostikale. *Metro: Casco Viejo, Tram: Mercado. Map 5, E3, p256* From some angles this bar looks like a British bed 'n' breakfast, while other views take in bizarre Botero frescoes. At weekends it's cheerfully packed, with locals unwinding to unchallenging music. Try to visit a toilet before showing up.

Muga, C Ronda 10. *Metro: Casco Viejo, Tram: Mercado. Map 5, D4, p256* A longstanding favourite, this relaxed café and bar has a rock 'n' roll vibe, with colourful tables, fanzines and CDs for sale, and a down-to-earth clientele.

Twiggy, Alameda de Urquijo 35. *Metro: Indautxu. Map 4, F9, p255* Psychedelic colours and a 1960s feel characterize this bar in one of the busiest weekend hubs.

Zulo, Barrenkale 22. *Metro: Casco Viejo, Tram: Arriaga. Map 5, E3, p256* A tiny nationalist bar with plenty of character. There's a bearded Bilbao personality called Txema behind the bar and a welcoming set, who definitely don't follow the Bill Clinton line on non-inhalation. The name means 'hole' or 'burrow'.

Clubs

Bullitt, C Dos de Mayo 3. *Metro: Casco Viejo, Tram: Mercado. Map 5, G1, p256* Across the river from the Casco Viejo, this disco-bar has a variety of music styles and is perhaps Bilbao's best nightlife venue. On Saturdays, it's Black Roots night, with excellent soul and R&B. Other nights offer ska, reggae and 1960s rock. It closes at 0130, or thereabouts, but at weekends it re-opens at 0630 as an 'afterhours' club and the action keeps going all morning.

Café Indie, C Doctor Areilza 34. *Metro: San Mamés, Tram: San Mamés. Map 4, H6, p254* Trendier and sleeker than the name might suggest, with sofas downstairs and a bar and dance floor upstairs. At weekends it makes some other clubs look empty, with both music and crowd that are suspiciously on the mainstream side of indie. British retro gets some play too.

Congreso, Muelle de Uribitarte 4. *Metro: Abando, Tram: Uribitarte. Map 2, B10, p255* A classic *bacalao* (Spanish techno) and house

Bars and clubs

venue, hardly cutting-edge but a mainstay of the Bilbao scene. The mixed crowd doesn't really get into its stride until 0400. Open Friday and Saturday only.

Conjunto Vacío, C Muelle de la Merced 4. *Metro: Casco Viejo, Tram: Mercado. Map 4, E12, p255* Empty by name and packed by nature, at least from about 0200 on Fridays and Saturdays. The music is fairly light *bacalao*; the crowd is mixed and good-looking; the drinks are horrendously expensive but the entry is free.

Distrito 9, Alameda Rekalde 18. *Metro: Moyúa, Tram: Guggenheim. Map 4, D7, p255* This is still probably the best spot in Bilbao for house music and is quite a dressy scene, with drag shows and a €10 cover. Open until very late. Mixed crowd.

El Balcón de la Lola, C Bailén 10. *Metro: Abando. Map 4, E12, p255* Decorated in industrial style with sheet-metal and graffiti, this is a good Saturday night club that varies in character from cheesy dance music to heavier stuff. Open until late; €5 at the door.

New Garden, C Lehendakari Aguirre 13, **T** 944-760056. *Metro: Deustu. Map 4, E1, p254* Below the Casa Vasca restaurant, this place has a double identity. During the week it features some fairly nostalgic music with older couples dancing. At weekends it fills with students and the pop goes on until late.

Santana 27, C Santana 27, Bolueta. *Metro: Bolueta.* Near the Metro station in Bolueta, this vast venue avoids the strict opening hours in central Bilbao and keeps on partying until 0600 (or later) every night. There are so many dance floors that you are bound to find something you like; it often hosts live bands and special club nights too. The €6 cover includes one drink.

East of Bilbao

Bars

Arrana, C Juan Calzada 6, Gernika. A vibrant Basque bar with a lively young crowd spilling outside at weekends.

Ku-Kua, Kanttoipe, Ondarroa. A very lively bar that gets very full and stays open until very late.

La Leñera, Mundaka. A friendly bar located in Mundaka's tiny backstreets. No *pintxos* but plenty of seats.

Metropol, C Unamuno and C Iparragirre, Gernika. A cavernous and comradely bar that's open later than anywhere else in town, and then some.

Sakris, Markina. In the backstreets of the old town, this tiny bar is housed in a 17th-century palace and is one of the more atmospheric choices in relaxed Markina.

Talako, Leikeitio. Located above the fishermen's co-operative on the harbour, this is a great spot for one of Lekeitio's rainy days, with a pool table, board games and a panoramic view of the harbour, town and beaches.

San Sebastián/Donostia

Bars

The Parte Vieja has many options. In Centro, calles Larramendi and Reyes Católicos near the cathedral are full of bars and there's student nightlife around Calle San Bartolomé, just back from the beach.

Altxerri Bar, C Reina Regenta 2. *Map 2, B5, p250* An atmospheric cellar bar next to the tourist office which regularly showcases live jazz and other acts. Draws an interesting crowd and is worth a visit even if there's nothing on.

Arkaitzpe, C Mayor 14, **T** 943-421867. *Map 2, B3, p250* A good bar, modern, blue and relaxed. Later at night the tables disappear and the dancing starts.

Arrauna, C Angel 2. *Map 2, B3, p250* In a quiet corner of the Parte Vieja, this is a committedly leftist Basque bar and a solid place to hole up when the weather closes in.

Bar El Cine, C San Bartolomé 21, **T** 943-460783. *Map 2, F3, p250* A long-standing student favourite in this busy zone. A massive complex with loud, cheesy music and several bars. Open until dawn at weekends.

Bar Ondarra, Av de la Zurriola 16. *Map 2, A7, p250* Opposite the Kursaal exhibition centre in Gros, this is a decent venue with a small, street-level bar serving good *pintxos*, and an underground den featuring regular live jazz and soul. It's a relaxed place to have a *copa*.

Be Bop, Paseo de Salamanca 3. *Map 2, B5, p250* This much-visited bar by the river mouth is quiet and relaxing and has regular live jazz sessions. Entry is usually about €5.

Bideluze, Pl Guipúzcoa 14. *Map 2, C5, p250* This is a lively and interesting bar, with two floors of eccentric furniture. Simple food is served downstairs and there are *pintxos* upstairs. It's popular with young and old; you may be addressed in Euskara.

El Nido, C Larramendi 13. *Map 2, F5, p250* A sizeable pub which doesn't empty until late. Friendly crowd and board games.

Etxekalte, C Mari 11. *Map 2, B3, p250* On the harbour side of the old town, this is a popular and atmospheric place to hang out on a Saturday night. The music is mostly jazz.

Garagar, Alameda del Boulevard 22, **T** 943-422840. *Map 2, B4, p250* Slightly overpriced pub at the edge of the Parte Vieja with some comfy booths. It keeps 'em pouring in until 0200 most nights (0400 at weekends), and it's much more relaxing than some of the other tourist-oriented late-openers. DJ upstairs at weekends.

Museo del Whisky, Alameda del Boulevard, **T** 943-426478, museo@telefonica.net. *Map 2, C4, p250* As good as its name, with over 3000 different bottles on site. It's a very relaxing place to sit back with a single malt, and there's a piano bar downstairs. The superb range of drams doesn't come cheap, however.

Soma 107, C Larramendi 4, **T** 943-468810. *Map 2, F5, p250* Relaxed place, almost terminally so, with marijuana posters and paraphernalia, Internet, books, food and two levels of seating. Sensitively decorated with cool murals, graffiti and paintings.

Clubs

Bataplán, Playa de la Concha s/n, **T** 943-460439. *Map 2, F2, p250* San Sebastián's most famous *discoteca* is right on La Concha beach. It's open Thursday to Saturday from midnight onwards and attracts a smart young crowd, with its mix of club anthems and pop crowd-pleasers. Rises to prominence during the film festival when it hosts various after-parties. €7-15 entry.

Discobolo, Alameda de Boulevard 27. *Map 2, C4, p250* A tacky option just outside Parte Vieja. It's far from cutting edge but the atmosphere is cheerful.

Kandela, C Escolta Real 20, Antiguo. This bar in the suburb of Antiguo usually features live bands from Thursday to Sunday. Music ranges from rock to pop and usually kicks off at about 2300. The €6 entry includes a drink.

Komplot, C Pedro Egaña 5, **T** 943-472109. *Map 2, C5, p250* Small and à la mode club featuring probably the best house music in San Sebastián. Just next to the Euskotren station.

Ku, Monte Igueldo s/n. On the Igueldo hill at the end of Ondarreta beach is one of the city's more glamorous discos, with a smart, mixed crowd. Usually goes on later than anywhere else.

La Kabutzia, Paseo de la Concha s/n, **T** 943-429785. *Map 2, C3, p250* Situated in the ship-like Real Club Naútico on the beach, this is a well-situated club with a young crowd.

Rotonda, Playa de la Concha 6, **T** 943-429095. *Map 2, F1, p250* Another club on La Concha beach, open very late weekend nights. The music on offer varies, but usually hovers around popular dance, with some salsa and reggae thrown in as required.

Inland from San Sebastián

Bars

Bar Irritz, C Zaharri, Oñati. A late-opening weekend bar on Oñati's main street offering popular techno and a friendly scene.

Parra Taberna, Elorrio. A peaceful bar with tables on the main square and a beautiful glass and stone interior.

Vitoria/Gasteiz

Bars

There are quite a few bars on calles Zapatería and Correría and around Plaza de la Burullería; most are only open at the weekend. There are also plenty of bars around calles San Francisco and Fueros. The old town tends to have boisterous, no-frills bars with a Basque atmosphere, while the new town has a more chic scene.

Bar Río, C Eduardo Dato 20, **T** 945-230067. A decent café with outdoor tables by day, this becomes one of the last bars to shut at night, when it caters to a good-natured gay and straight crowd. There's original live music on Thursday nights.

Café Iguana, Correría 94, **T** 945-122837. This recently opened spot has a great ambience. Plenty of tables, well-mixed drinks and a friendly crowd of arty people make it ideal for an after-dinner *copa* . One of Vitoria's best.

El Bodegón de Gorbea, C Herrería 26, on the corner of Cantón San Roque. A classic, no-frills bar with rock music, cheap beer and a bohemian bunch of friendly Basques, chatting and drinking from early until very late.

Gora, Cantón de San Francisco Javier. A modern, spacious place just off Calle Cuchillería, with whimsical decor depicting an executive pulling off his work clothes. Green, light and peaceful.

Hala Bedi, C Cuchillería 98, **T** 945-260411. A late-opening Basque bar with a cheerful atmosphere, serving delicious crêpes.

Clubs

Aural, C Paseo de la Senda 2, **T** 945-147400. A fairly refined club as these things go, with a very trendy interior and chart hits alongside a fair whack of nostalgia. Attracts a more mature crowd than many.

Cairo Stereo Club, C Aldabe 9. Great Vitorian club with some excellent and innovative DJs and a mixed crowd. During the week it often shows cult movies or holds theme parties.

Chip, C Prudencio María Verástegui 9, **T** 945-256561. Just next to the Artium, this *discoteca* is popular with a thirty-something crowd. It's relaxed, pleasant and not too loud or crowded. Open Friday to Sunday only.

Gallery, Pl San Antón 4, **T** 945-250502. A young and lively set of punters makes this a good place to come for *bacalao* and house.

Pravda, C Guerrillero Fernández de Leceta 7. This grungy and small underground venue is popular with a young, spaced-out crowd. Music tends towards trance. The busiest night is Saturday.

Swing, C Bastiturri 1, **T** 945-281372. A reasonable club that doesn't veer much from the comfortable pop and techno line. Mixed crowd with a strong lesbian scene.

Tapioca, C Sancho El Sabio 22, **T** 945-247471. A relaxed and fairly funky club with music from soul through to soft house. The interesting decor includes exhibitions by young local artists. It's open until 0500 at weekends.

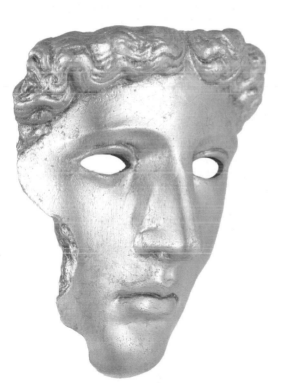

Cinema

Nearly all foreign films shown in the Basque country are dubbed. There's significant resistance in Spain to subtitles, which springs not least from the dubbers themselves, who have a relatively lucrative career laid out if one of the actors whose lines they speak makes it big in Hollywood. If your Spanish is so-so, it's usually easier to understand original Spanish films than dubbed ones; being able to read the lips is a big help. Nearly all screenings cost around the €6 mark, sometimes discounted for earlier shows or quieter nights. Typical show times are 1700, 2000 and 2230.

Bilbao

Cinema Mikeldi, Alameda Urquijo 66, El Ensanche, **T** 944-411728. *Metro: Indautxu. Map 4, G7, p255* A smallish but convenient cinema on Plaza Indautxu, showing major releases.

Cines Avenida, C Lehendakari Aguirre 18, Deusto, **T** 944-757796. *Metro: Deustu. Map 4, D1, p254* This is one of the better cinemas around and tends to show a few lower-profile releases and arthouse films, as well as some Basque pictures.

Cines Capitol, C Villarías 10, El Ensanche, **T** 944-310310. *Metro: Abando, Tram: Ayuntamiento Map 4, C11, p255* The handiest cinema for the Casco Viejo, just across the river.

Cines Multis, C José María Escuza 13, El Ensanche. *Metro/Tram: San Mamés. Map 4, H5, p254* This complex has more interesting releases than some and also more Spanish-language pictures.

Ideal Cinema, C Egaña 1, **T** 944-210561, El Ensanche. *Metro: Indautxu. Map 4, G10, p255* Large complex near Plaza Zabálburu that shows big releases but also hosts some short topical festivals.

Lauren Getxo Zinemak, Muelle Arriluce s/n, Getxo. *Metro: Neguri*. A big complex with a dozen screens, on the pier in Getxo, showing standard Hollywood fare.

San Sebastián

Antzoki Zaharra, C Mayor 3, Parte Vieja, **T** 943-426112. *Map 2, B3, p250* This auditorium showcases offbeat cinema and theatre.

Cines Principe, C San Juan 8-12, Parte Vieja. *Map 2, A4, p250* A large, central cinema opposite the San Telmo museum.

Cines Trueba, Pl Espnola s/n, Gros. *Map 2, B7, p250* One of the only cinemas in the Basque country to show regular *versión original* English-language films.

Vitoria

Cines Florida, C San Prudencio 24. Very large and central Vitorian cinema with a variety of films on offer.

Cines Guridi, C San Prudencio 6. Between them, this and the allied Florida cover plenty of bases.

Music

Opera and classical performances are alive and kicking in all three of the Basque cities, boosted by the opening of the Kursaal and the Euskalduna. Fiestas aside, there isn't a huge scene in popular live music but there are several good venues in each place. The notable exception is Basque rock, whose real home is in the smaller towns of Euskadi – particularly Ondarroa. It's guaranteed that, wherever the pro-independence posters are concentrated, there'll be a local band banging out some anthemic songs of freedom.

Bilbao

For regular opera performances, see **Teatro Arriaga**, p196.

Cotton Club, C Gregorio de la Revilla 25. *Metro: Indautxu. Map 4, H7, p255* A live music venue with a relaxed atmosphere, Cotton Club is popular with a fairly upmarket crowd. It's decorated with trappings from the world of showbiz and hosts music ranging from rock to jazz. Open daily until late.

Kafe Antzokia, C San Vicente 2, **T** 944-244625, www.kafe antzokia.com. *Metro: Abando, Tram: Casino. Map 4, C10, p255* An ex-cinema turned Bilbao icon, this is a live venue for anything from death metal to Euskara poetry, and features two spacious floors with bars that serve until late at weekends. Sociable, friendly and loud: a place where you might hear more Euskara than Spanish.

Palacio Euskalduna, C Abandoibarra 4, **T** 944-310310. *Euskotren: Abandoibarra, Metro: San Mamés. Map 4, F3, p254* Top-quality classical performances from the symphonic orchestras of Bilbao and Euskadi, as well as high-profile Spanish and international artists.

East of Bilbao

Many bars in Ondarroa are temples to Basque rock, which is closely identified with the independence movement. The **Music School**, on the corner of calles Iñaki Deunaren and Sabino Arana (Arana'tar Sabin), often has live Basque alternative rock on Friday or Saturday nights; it's usually free and worth a look, especially as a contrast to Spanish music as a whole. Calle Nasa Kalea is also well-stocked with music bars: two worth dropping in on are **Apallu**, at number 30, and **Sansonategi**.

San Sebastián

For live jazz, see also **Altxerri Bar**, p186 and **Be Bop**, p186.

Kandela, C Escolta Real 20, Antiguo. *Map 1, E2, p218* This bar in the suburb of Antiguo usually features live bands from Thursday to Sunday. Music ranges from rock to pop and usually kicks off at about 2300. The €6 entry includes a drink.

Kursaal, Av Zurriola 1, Gros, **T** 943-003000. *Map 2, A6, p250* San Sebastián's architectural pride and joy hosts world-class classical concerts and opera.

Vitoria

Concerts and opera are held at the **Teatro Antzokia**, see p196.

Performing arts

After a fallow period during Franco's lengthy tenure, professional theatre in the Basque country has now taken its rightful place as a vehicle of Basque expression. Performances are frequently one-offs or on very short runs but are typically energetic, imaginative and avant-garde. A huge range of shows is presented even in the larger theatres; there's a seriously exploratory spirit that is very invigorating, even if it occasionally strays into the politically naïve.

Euskadi is also a great place for contemporary dance. Local troupes adapt traditional Basque dances, while styles from further afield, such as *flamenco*, can also be seen. There are few dedicated dance venues but most of the theatres devote a good portion of their programming to this art form. Ballet isn't the big thing in these parts; check the Arriaga in Bilbao or the Kursaal in San Sebastián for any that might be on.

Bilbao

La Fundición, C Francisco Macía 1, Deusto, **T** 944-753327. *Metro: Deustu. Map 4, D2, p254* Just across the Deusto bridge, this small set-up puts on fascinating dance shows from around the globe, as well as some excellent theatre from small companies.

Teatro Arriaga, Pl Arriaga 1, El Ensanche, **T** 944-792036, www.teatroarriaga.com. *Metro: Abando/Casco Viejo. Map 4, D12, p255* Bilbao's highest-profile theatre is picturesquely set on the river by the Casco Viejo. It's a plush venue in late-19th-century style but the work it presents can be very innovative. The better seats go for €25 and above but there are often decent pews available for €4-5. The box office is open during normal business hours.

Teatro Ayala, C Manuel Allende 18, El Ensanche, **T** 944-212260. *Metro: Indautxu. Map 4, H7, p255* Bilbao's second major theatre has slightly more conservative programming than the Arriaga.

Teatro Barakaldo, C Juán Sebastián Elkano 4, **T** 944-780600. *Metro: Barakaldo.* In the *barrio* of Barakaldo, this theatre presents a diverse progamme of local and touring theatre, music and dance.

San Sebastián

The main theatre, the beautiful **Victoria Eugenia**, has been under long-term restoration but should re-open in spring 2007. See also **Antzoki Zaharra**, p193.

Vitoria

Teatro Antzokia, C San Prudencio 29, Vitoria, **T** 945-161045. Vitoria's principal theatre has a blink-or-you'll-miss-it programme of a good variety of shows.

If the sun rises in the east, it's a sure sign that there's a festival taking place somewhere in Euskadi. Even the smallest village has its day (or week) of celebration. Although there are also modern cultural festivals, focusing on music or cinema, the majority are traditional and have a religious basis that, in many cases, pre-dates Christianity. Fiestas in larger towns will usually feature *corridas* or other bull-sports, as well as live music, markets and street performances. There's usually a procession (or six) and even the comedic ones usually have a symbolic significance, so it's worth asking around to find the meaning behind the figures. Whatever the occasion, whatever the weather, young and old will gather on the streets, slurp *kalimotxo* (red wine mixed with cola), and take riotous advantage of the bars, which usually stay open all night. It's difficult to find hotel rooms during fiestas but, if it comes to the worst, lock your bags in the bus or train station and make a night of it. And remember, if you stumble across the annual fiesta in a tiny village, it's likely to be just as quirky and exciting as the best-organized Bilbao showpiece.

January

Tamborrada (19-20 Jan), San Sebastián. The day of the 'pincushion saint' is celebrated with a deafening parade of drummers through the streets. It's said that the custom originated around the town well, when a group of local lasses started banging on the buckets they were waiting to fill. Many of the drummers are members of the city's gastronomic societies and dress as chefs; they adjourn to the kitchen after the parade to prepare the mother of all midnight feasts.

San Anastasio (22 Jan), Oyon. The Riojan town celebrates this saint's day by parading a figure named Katxi through the streets.

February

Carnaval usually kicks off on the Saturday before Ash Wednesday, and runs until Shrove Tuesday (47 days before Easter Sunday). There are celebrations throughout the region: San Sebastián, Bilbao and Vitoria are buzzing for the whole period and the Sunday festivities in Tolosa are considered the liveliest in Euskadi. More traditional carnivals can be seen in smaller towns such as Salvatierra, Zalduondo and Markina.

March/April

Semana Santa (Easter week). Bilbao marks the occasion with a number of serious hooded processions, accompanied by mournful drums and cornets, from Good Friday onwards. One of the best-known events is in the western Vizcayan town of Balmaseda, where the Stations of the Cross are re-enacted by residents. The person who is to play Christ begins to study the role three years in advance. Hondarribia puts on a similar play, while in the village of Salinas de Añana, villagers enact the mock trial and execution of Judas (see p111).

San Telmo (1st Sun after Easter), Zumaia. An *encierro* (running of bulls) is held on the beach to celebrate the saint's day.

San Prudencio (28 Apr). Celebrated with *tamborradas* throughout Alava. In Vitoria there is a re-enactment of the saint's life the night before.

May/June

Pentecost (7 weeks after Easter), Bergara. A town fiesta, with bull-sports, concerts and a *corrida*.

Corpus Christi (Thu after Trinity Sunday, 8 weeks after Easter). Festivities in many towns, notably Oñati, where there is traditional religious Basque dancing, notably the *espata dantza* (sword dance).

Getxo Blues Festival (2nd week of Jun). This international music festival is held in the Plaza Santa Eugenia, in Getxo.

San Juan (24 Jun) has his day in the sun in many places, notably Tolosa and Laguardia. The night before, bonfires are lit in many villages, echoing pre-Christian summer solstice celebrations.

Semana Gastronómica (last week of Jun), San Sebastián. A treat for the taste buds.

San Pedro (29 Jun). Celebrated particularly in Lekeitio, where the tricky *kaxarranka* is danced on top of a chest hoisted to shoulder height and carried around town.

July

High-profile **jazz festivals** are held in Getxo (1st week), Vitoria (3rd week) and San Sebastián (2nd fortnight).

Virgen del Carmen (16 Jul). Effigies of the Lady are carried out to sea in a procession of fishing boats at Plentzia and Santurtzi.

La Magdalena (22 Jul), Bermeo. Nautical events and races.

Santiago (25 Jul) is celebrated around the region but particularly in Vitoria on the **Día del Blusa** (blouse day) when colourfully dressed kids patrol the streets. Hondarribia celebrates with a procession from the fishermen's guild to the local church.

International Paella Competition (25 Jul), Getxo.

San Pedro (29 Jul), Mundaka. Traditional dancing

San Ignacio (31 Jul) is celebrated in Loiola and Getxo.

August
This is the most prolific month for Basque festivals; you could spend nearly the whole of August partying.

Virgen Blanca (4-9 Aug), Vitoria. The city's major knees-up.

San Salvador (7 Aug), Getaria. A re-enactment of the return of Elkano is staged every four years (next one in 2007).

San Nicolás (12 Aug), Getxo.

Aste Nagusia (Semana Grande: 9-15 Aug in San Sebastián; Sat-Fri after the 15 Aug in Bilbao). Firework displays in San Sebastián. Concerts, *corridas*, Basque sports and serious drinking in Bilbao. Major fiestas in Gernika and Markina on the 15th and 16th.

Fiesta de 31 de Agosto (31 Aug). San Sebastián tempts fate by commemorating the Great Fire of 1813, with hundreds of candles.

September

Euskal Jaiak (1st week), San Sebastián. A celebration of Basque crafts, culture and food. Yet another excuse to stuff yourself. A similar celebration takes place in Zarautz on the 9 September.

International Folk Festival (1st week), Getxo.

San Antolín (4 Sep), Lekeitio's seriously odd goose festival, p74.

Virgen de Guadalupe (8 Sep) Hondarribia. Commemorates the virgin's decisive intervention in a 1639 battle.

International Film Festival (3rd week), San Sebastián.

San Miguel (29 Sep), Oñati and Markina. Celebrated with dancing and plenty of consumption of the beverage bearing his name.

October/November

Early October is harvest time in the Rioja Alavesa, a happy season with many celebrations. An **international theatre festival** in Vitoria lasts from October to December.

December

Advent (1-24 Dec). Vitoria is known for its spectacular full-sized nativity scene, with over 200 figures. On the weekend before Christmas, the character Olentzero, a charcoal seller, announces the approach of Christmas in Basque towns and villages. On Christmas Eve the citizens of San Sebastián climb Monte Igueldo with an effigy of a *besugo* (sea bream), and an open-air midnight mass is held by firelight in Labastida in the Rioja Alavesa.

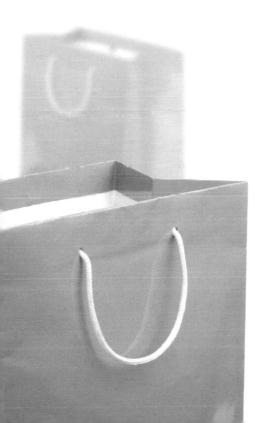

Shopping

Bilbao is by far the best place to shop in the Basque region; San Sebastián and Vitoria have their share of stores but there's a wider range and more quirky options in the bigger city. Business hours vary, but shops normally open up at 0930 or 1000, break for lunch at 1400, come back at 1700, and stay open until 2000 or 2030. Most shops are open on Saturday mornings and many clothes shops are open all weekend. The advent of the euro resulted in some sharp price increases, so Spain isn't as cheap as it once was. That said, wine is still better value than in the UK, and spirits are much, much cheaper (although taxes surely won't stay low for long). Clothes are by no means cheap in the Basque country but there are a number of well-priced Spanish brands that don't have outlets elsewhere and are worth investigating. Delicatessen goods, such as ham, cheese and olive oil, are also good purchases. Most towns and villages have a weekly food and clothing market where it is possible to bargain on non-food items.

Bilbao/Bilbo

The city's new shopping centre, **Zubiarte**, is the sort of temple to commerce that is killing old shopping quarters all across Spain. It's just beyond the Guggenheim by the Puente de Deusto (Tram: Abandoibarra), and has fashion outlets, eateries and a cinema.

Books and music

Tipo, C Somera 39, Casco Viejo. *Map 5, E4, p256* Decent record shop with a fair alternative section.

Topbooks, Gran Vía 22, El Ensanche. *Map 4, D9, p255* One of the larger bookshops in town, with a fair selection of Spanish, Euskara and English titles.

Department stores

Corte Inglés, Gran Vía 7, El Ensanche, **T** 944-253500. *Mon-Sat until 2200. Map 4, D10, p255* The usual several floors of everything. Also at Calle La Paz in Vitoria, **T** 945-266333.

Clothing and fashion

Adolfo Dominguez, C Arias 16, El Ensanche. *Map 4, F7, p255* Selection of smartish casual to semi-formal men's clothing. Stylish and fairly pricey.

Amsterdam Plein, C Askao 2 and Pl Nueva, Casco Viejo. *Map 5, C3, p256* Individual clothing for the young alternative set.

Bershka, C Arias 17, El Ensanche. *Map 4, F8, p255* A warehouse-sized depository for some Britney-trendy clothes for teens and young women.

Falstaff, C Colón de Larreátegui 29, El Ensanche. *Map 4, D9, p255* Despite the name, this sells some pretty original clothing for young-at-heart women.

Gorostiaga, C Victor s/n, Casco Viejo. *Map 5, D2, p256* A serious hat shop, selling all a Basque could desire, including berets.

Kukuxumusu, C Arias 27, El Ensanche. *Map 4, F7, p255* A happy shop, with a range of cheerful Basque T-shirts in bright colours.

Trantxo, C Somera 8, Casco Viejo. *Map 5, E4, p256* Alternative fashion on this alternative street.

Wakalouka, C Diputación 4, El Ensanche. *Map 4, E9, p255* Everything you'll need to get into the Basque surfing scene, plus snow gear.

Crafts, gifts and souvenirs

On Sundays Bilbao has a small, quirky flea market in the Plaza Nueva and a bigger one at Bolueta (Metro: Bolueta).

Athletic Bilbao, Alameda Rekalde 44, El Ensanche. *Map 4, F8, p255* Also at C Bidebarrieta 10, Casco Viejo. *Map 5, E2, p256* Your one-stop shop for all souvenirs relating to Los Leones. If it's not red and white, it's not here.

Barandiaran, C Navarra 1, El Ensanche. *Map 4, C11, p255* Approaching its 100th year, this old-fashioned perfume shop is still going strong.

Bilbo Carnaval, C Artekale and C Tendería, Casco Viejo. *Map 5, E3, p256* A selection of dolls and costumes guaranteed to get you into the pre-Lenten spirit.

El Rastrillo, C Iparraguirre 42, El Ensanche. *Map 4, G8, p255*
Characterful second-hand barn selling everything, including
several kitchen sinks.

Gaston y Daniela, C Correo and C Cinturería, Casco Viejo. *Map 5,
E3, p256* A beautifully painted building houses this venerable
carpet and fabric chain in the heart of the old town.

Hobby's, Gran Vía 57, El Ensanche. *Map 4, F6, p254* Recreate the
siege of Bilbao in Airfix or build a Basque fishing trawler from little
pieces. The toy soldiers include figures of Hitler and Mussolini.

Intermon, Alameda Urquijo 11, El Ensanche. *Map 4, F10, p255*
An eclectic mix of handcrafts with the emphasis on fair trade.
There are items from the everyday to the fanciful.

Txorrerri, C Artekale 25, Casco Viejo. *Map 5, E4, p256* A nice little
shop peddling home-made honey and other cottage products.

Food and drink

Arreser, Gran Vía 24, El Ensanche. *Map 4, D9, p255* A historic
pastelería, with an intriguing selection of cakes and sweeties.

Chocolates de Mendaro, C Licenciado Poza 14, El Ensanche.
Map 4, F8, p255 A tiny shop selling boutique chocolates that
are just too gorgeous to eat... maybe.

Claudio, C Esperanza 48, El Arenal. *Map 5, B1, p256* Respected
shop dealing in cured pigs' legs. Try before you buy.

Ibeas, C Licenciado Poza 27, El Ensanche. *Map 4, G7, p255*
A classy shop selling a range of good wines, spirits and gourmet
deli products, as well as wrapped gifts and hampers.

Mercado de la Ribera, C Ribera s/n, Casco Viejo. *Map 5, F3, p256* Three floors of produce on the edge of the old town (see p39).

Oka, C Colón de Larreátegui 33 and C Marqués del Puerto, El Ensanche. *Map 4, D8, p255* A small but excellent corner deli, particularly strong on cheese but with some good *jamones*, too.

El País Vasco/Euskadi

Casa del Libro, C Arka 11, Vitoria, **T** 945-158175. *Daily 0930-2030*. A comprehensive bookshop with plenty of English titles.

Donosti-Rock, C 31 de Agosto 3, San Sebastián, **T** 943-423937. *Map 2, A4, p250* Great shop for the heavier and darker end of the music spectrum.

Graphos, C Mayor 1, San Sebastián, **T** 943-426377. *Map 2, C3, p250* On the edge of the old town, this has an excellent selection of maps of the region.

Frudisk, C Miracruz 6, San Sebastián. *Map 2, C7, p250* A decent Gros music shop that also has internet access.

La Bretxa, Pl de Bretxa, San Sebastián. *Map 2, B4, p250* Market complex in the old town (see p86).

Segunda Mano, C Prudencio María Verástegui 14, Vitoria, **T** 945-270007. An amazing barn-sized second-hand shop, with everything from books to grand pianos and skis to confessionals.

Sport is big in the Basque lands. Football is an obsession and strongly connected to the political situation: a win for Athletic Bilbao over Real Madrid, the darlings of the Spanish establishment, carries meaning far beyond the pitch. Great importance is also placed on traditional Basque sports, best seen at village fiestas. These tend to be fairly unreconstructed tests of strength, such as wood-chopping or stone-lifting, in which stocky *harrijasotzaileak* dead-lift weights which can exceed 300 kg; you can almost feel the hernias popping out. The best known Basque sport, however, is *pelota* or *jai alai*, played on a three-sided court. In the most common version, two teams of two hit the ball with their hands against the walls, seeking to prevent the other team from returning it. The ball is far from soft and, after a long career, players' hands resemble winning entries in a root-vegetable show. Variations of the game are *pelota a pala*, using bats and *cesta punta*, using a wickerwork glove that can propel the ball at frightening speeds.

Adventure activities

With its long coast and green hills, Euskadi is made for outdoor activities. Cycling, horse trekking, watersports and walking are well-catered for and rewarding. There are several adventure tourism organizations offering a range of activities across the provinces. Tourist offices have a full list but some of the best are:

Euskal Abentura, C Salvador 16, Bilbao, **T** 656-728085, www.euskalabenturaelkartea.net An adventure company organizing a massive range of activities throughout Euskadi.

Getxo Abentura An initiative of the Getxo tourist office, **T** 944-910800, www.getxo.net. Organizes just about any outdoor activity in the area, from caving to canoeing.

Ludoland, C Herrería 25, Vitoria, **T** 902-293000, www.ludoland.net. Offers all manner of outdoor pursuits, including skiing, rafting, canyoning, hiking.

Troka Abentura, C Zabalbide 26, Bilbao, **T** 944-334728, www.troka.com. Bungee jumping, abseiling, caving, mountain biking and hot-air balloon rides.

Tura, based at the tourist office in Salvatierra, **T** 945-312535, www.tura.org. Organizes a range of outdoor activities throughout Alava province.

Bullfighting

Bullfighting is big during the summer fiestas. **Bilbao** (see p52) is the best place to see a *corrida* but tickets are tricky to get. Many of the small towns have *corridas* and other bovine events during their fiestas, one involves teams of two attempting to put brass rings on a cow's horns. **Zumaia** celebrates the festival of San Telmo, with an *encierro* (running of the bulls) on the beach.

Cycling

Cycling is very popular. When the professional circuit comes to the region, the roads become full of enthused *cuadrillas* of friends, racing each other through the rural landscape. Miguel Indurain, one of the greatest road cyclists of all time and winner of five consecutive Tours de France, was born in neighbouring Navarra.

Federación Vasca de Ciclismo, Paseo Anoeta 12, San Sebastián, **T** 943-457069, www.fvascicli.com. The controlling body for cycling in Euskadi is very helpful for all things two-wheeled.

Football

For information on **Athletic Bilbao**, see p52 and p213.

San Sebastián's football team, **Real Sociedad** (**T** 943-462833, **F** 458941, www.real-sociedad-sad.es) plays at the Estadio de Anoeta, Paseo de Anoeta 1. Matches are usually held at 1700 on Sunday but check the website or www.marca.es for upcoming fixtures. Tickets (€24-39) are sold at the stadium from Thursday to Saturday and two hours before kick-off on Sunday. The club was given its royal title in 1910 and is one of few to have won the Spanish league title twice running (in 1981 and 1982).

The third major team in the Basque country is **Deportivo Alavés** (**T** 945-131018, www.alaves.com), Vitoria's side, who yo-yo between the *Primera* and *Segunda*. They play at the chilly Mendizorroza stadium, a couple of blocks southwest of the Parque del Prado.

Horse racing

Hipódromo, C Camino, southeast of San Sebastián, **T** 943-423698, www.donostiasansebastian.com/hipodromo. The short but high-quality racing season is in April and May.

▶ Athletic Bilbao

So this Bilbaíno is in a bar chatting with a friend and asks him: "Did you hear that they've spent 100 million on El Guggenheim?"

The friend thinks for a while: "Well, as long as he bangs in a few goals that's not too bad…"

Rarely has a football team been loved as deeply as Athletic Club. A Basque symbol in the same league as the Gernika oak, the team, as a matter of principle, only fields Basque players. Astonishingly, it has remained very competitive in what is arguably the strongest league in the world and has never been relegated (although at time of publication it was in serious danger of the drop). Athletic Bilbao has won the Spanish Cup 24 times and the Championship eight times, more than any other club bar the two Madrid giants and Barcelona.

Athletic Club grew out of the cultural exchange that was taking place in the late 19th century between Bilbao and the UK. British workers and miners brought football to Bilbao and the Basques went to Britain to study engineering. In the early years, Athletic fielded many British players and their strip was modelled on the colours worn by Sunderland FC.

Games are usually held on Sundays at 1700 (see p52).

(see p52)

Sports

Horse riding

There are several riding schools in the Basque region. Alava is the best province for trekking on horseback. Tourist offices will provide details, or try:

Artziniega Rutas a Caballo, T 945-396060. Alavan organization specializing in trekking expeditions.

Club Hípico Okendo, **T** 945-898098. Another Alavan riding club organizing excursions.

Pelota

Federación Vasca de Pelota, **T** 946-818108, www.euskal pilota.com. The controlling body for all *pelota* in Euskadi has a website that lists upcoming events in slightly shambolic fashion. Most courts have matches on Saturday and Sunday evenings. Confusingly, the seasons vary from town to town but there's always something on somewhere.

Watersports

Federación Vasca de Surf, C Julián Gaiarre 44, Bilbao, **T** 944-735125, www.euskalsurf.com. The Basque surf federation has plenty of information, including a list of surf schools and surf clubs.

K-Sub, C Trinidad 2, Zarautz, **T/F** 943-132472, runs PADI scuba-diving courses.

Maremoto Renting, Puerto Deportivo de Getxo, **T** 944-606503, rents out jet skis and sailboards, and runs trips.

Mundaka Surf Shop, Paseo de Txorrokopunta 10, Mundaka, **T** 946-876721, www.mundakasurfshop.com. A great source of information, as well as a place to hire or buy any surf-related gear. It also runs beginners' classes in summer.

Náutica Getxo, Puerto Deportivo de Getxo, **T** 609 985 977. Yachts, with or without a skipper, can be chartered from the jetty at the end of Ereaga beach.

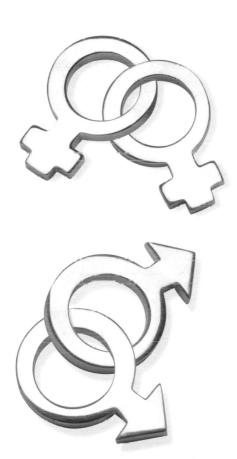

Euskadi's political awareness and antipathy to Spanish conservatism means that the Basque cities are among the most tolerant in the peninsula. While there's not a gay scene to compare with Barcelona or Madrid, there are plenty of gay and lesbian venues and several dedicated organizations. Overt displays of homophobia are rare and couples on the street shouldn't encounter any problems, at least in urban areas. Bilbao has the busiest and best scene of the three and has experienced a dramatic increase in gay tourism since the opening of the Guggenheim. San Sebastián, particularly in summer, also sees plenty of activity. Vitoria is quieter but still has a handful of places to go.

The principal gay and lesbian organization in Euskadi is **EHGAM**, C Dos de Mayo 8 (corner of C Lamana), Bilbao, **T** 944-150719, which can help with any information on gay and lesbian culture and life in Euskadi. Also check out **Aldarte**, C Barroeta Aldamar 7, Bilbao, **T** 944-237296, a resource centre that offers information, social events and support.

Bilbao

The 'pink zone' in Bilbao is across the river from the Casco Viejo near the Puente de la Merced. The Casco Viejo also has a few options. The major zone for cruising is the Parque de Doña Casilda, near the pergola; in summer, the Bosque de Azkorri in Getxo and Artxanda are also popular. In addition to the venues listed here, **Bizitza**, **Café Lamiak** and **Distrito 9** are popular, gay-friendly venues, see p181 and p184.

Badulake, C Hernani 10. *Metro: Casco Viejo, Tram: Arriaga. Map 5, G1, p256* A bar that hosts weekend cabaret shows and other events. Lesbian-oriented but all welcome. €3 entry after 0200 at weekends.

Element, C Costa s/n, off Av General Concha, **T** 944-052303, www.element.es. *€6 Thu, €10 Fri Sun. Metro: Moyúa. Map 4, E5, p254* This is by far the best of Bilbao's saunas. It's open on Thursday and Friday evenings and all day at the weekends, including late on Friday and Saturday nights.

El Santu Bear, C Dos de Mayo 8 and C Lamana. *Metro: Casco Viejo, Tram: Arriaga. Map 4, E12, p255* A relaxed and friendly bar that's not only confined to bears. It has a dark room but, apparently, it can be pretty chilly in there. The EHGAM office is located upstairs.

Heaven, C Dos De Mayo 4. *Metro: Casco Viejo, Tram: Arriaga. Map 4, E12, p255* A men-only bar with loud dance music that carries on until late. There's a lounge area and a *cuarto oscuro* (dark room) behind the main bar.

High, C Naja s/n. *Metro: Casco Viejo, Tram: Arriaga. Map 4, E12, p255* One of the best gay bars in this zone, just across the bridge from the Casco Viejo. It has a dark room and is open every day until pretty late. Entry is €5, which includes a drink.

Gay and lesbian

Holl-Berri, C Amistad 6. *Metro: Abando. Map 4, C11, p255* Near the station, a popular spot for drinking, dancing and cruising.

Mykonos, C General Castillo 4. *Metro: Casco Viejo, Tram: Arriaga. Map 4, F12, p255* Another pink zone option with back room and video lounge.

Txokolanda, Escalinata de Solokoetxe 4. *Metro: Casco Viejo; Tram: Ribera. Map 5, E4, p256* A fairly quiet but pleasant bar at the edge of the old town. Run by good people.

San Sebastián

Check out **Ku** on Monte Igueldo (see p188), which attracts a glammed-up, mixed crowd and is open later than anywhere else. **La Pluma** (C Sánchez Toca 5) is a popular bar in the Reyes Católicos bar zone with a girls-only night.

Vitoria

Bar Río (p189) is a pleasant café and late-night bar that attracts a good-natured gay and straight crowd. Mixed clubs (see p190) include **Cairo Stereo Club**, **Tapioca** and **Swing**; the last is the city's main lesbian club.

Kids are kings in Spain and Euskadi is no exception. They are a highly recommended travel accessory to ensure that you get friendly service, tables in full restaurants and much more. There's never a problem taking children anywhere; the locals do. It's usual for children to accompany parents on a Friday night out; you'll often see them playing in and out of bars at two in the morning.

The most enjoyable city in Euskadi for children is San Sebastián. The relaxed atmosphere, long beachfront and pedestrian old town all make for a hassle-free holiday. Bilbao has less to offer younger children but the seaside isn't far and the castle of Butrón will intrigue. It's worth staying in the Casco Viejo, which is free from traffic except in the mornings.

★ Best

Beaches for kids

- Laida, near Mundaka, has shallow water and golden sand, p67.
- Arrigorri is Ondarroa's best beach, with gentle waves, p77.
- Malkorbe, near Getaria, is sheltered by the *'ratón'*, p78.
- Ondarreta in San Sebastián is sheltered and has a playground and swimming pools for kids, p90.
- Hondarribia's gentle waters are popular with families, p98.

Bilbao/Bilbo

Artxanda, p42   Ride the red funicular to this picnic spot overlooking the city.

Athletic Bilbao, p52   Bilbao's football team plays to a colourful crowd. The atmosphere is fabulous and very family-orientated.

Casco Viejo, p33   The evening street life in the old town is fascinating, with plenty of buskers, living statues and a family atmosphere.

Castillo Butrón, p61   This fairytale castle just outside Bilbao has all the essential elements of a medieval fortress and is stocked with mannequins to bring the atmosphere to life.

Guggenheim, p43   The tactile building will appeal to children and the museum also runs child-friendly tours and workshops at weekends; check the website for upcoming dates.

Puente de Vizcaya, p58   The transporter bridge is very cool and the walkway 50 m above gives great views over the estuary; it is safe for all pre-vertigo ages.

Kids

There's a traditional merry-go-round on the beachfront at San Sebastián.

San Sebastián/Donostia

Aquarium, p83 The walk-through tank is fascinating, sharks get fed twice daily and the ghostly stingrays are equally watchable.

Kutxaespacio, p95 The hands-on science museum has plenty of things to push and pull, as well as computer activities. The attached planetarium is a good show but phone ahead to beat the queues.

Monte Igueldo, p90 Catch the funicular up the hill to enjoy a traditional funfair, a haunted house and great views.

Directory

Airline offices

British Airways, Aeropuerto de Bilbao, **T** 944-710523. **Iberia**, C Ercilla 20, Bilbao, **T** 944-245506; C Bengoetxea 3, San Sebastián, **T** 943-423586; Av Gasteiz 84, Vitoria, **T** 945-224142. **Spanair**, Aeropuerto de Bilbao, **T** 944-869498.

Banks and ATMs

All ATMs accept most international debit and credit cards. Banking hours are generally Mon-Fri 0830-1400 in summer and Mon-Sat 0830-1400 in winter. Most banks will exchange foreign currency although rates of commission vary widely.

Bicycle hire

The best place to hire bikes (and motorcycles) in Bilbao is **Alquimoto**, C Anselma de Salces 9, **T** 944-012563, www.alquimoto.com, bikes start from €7.50 per day. The **youth hostel**, p132, and the **Hotel Nervión**, p128, rent out bikes to their guests and might be persuaded to let non-guests use the facility. **Bici Rent Donosti**, Av de la Zurriola 22, San Sebastián, **T** 943-290854, 655724458, open daily from 0900 till 2100, rents bikes from its shop on Gros beach by the hour and by the day. They're not cheap at €18 per day, but there's a decent range, and the staff will help with planning trips, etc. **Ludoland**, C Herrería 25, Vitoria, **T** 945-122198, €10 per day but the bikes are often all gone early in the day.

Car hire

Check internet sites like www.webcarhire.com for substantial savings when booking a car rental.

    Atesa, C Sabino Arana 9, Bilbao, **T** 944-423290; Aeropuerto de Bilbao, **T** 944-533340; Portal de Betoño 11, Vitoria, **T** 945-271012, www.atesa.es. **Avis**, Av Doctor Areilza 34, Bilbao, **T** 944-275760, Aeropuerto de Bilbao, **T** 944-869648; C Triunfo 2, San Sebastián, **T** 943-461556; Av Gasteiz, Vitoria, **T** 945-247783, www.avis.com.

Europcar, Av Licenciado Poza 56, **T** 944-422226; Aeropuerto de Bilbao, **T** 944-710133; Estación del Norte, San Sebastián, **T** 943-322304; C Adriano VI 29, Vitoria, **T** 945-200433, www.europcar.com. **Hertz**, C Doctor Achucarro 10, Bilbao, **T** 944-153677; Aeropuerto de Bilbao, **T** 944-530931; C Zubieta 5, San Sebastián, **T** 943-461084; Pasaje de las Antillas 12, Vitoria, **T** 945200168, www.hertz.com.

Consulates
Britain, **T** 944-157600. **Eire**, **T** 944-912575. **France**, **T** 944-249000. **Germany**, **T** 944-238585. **Portugal**, **T** 944-354540. **South Africa**, **T** 944-641124. **US Embassy in Madrid**, **T** 915-872200

Credit card lines
Amex, **T** 902-375637. **Mastercard**, **T** 900-971231. **Visa**, **T** 900-951125.

Disabled
Bidaideak, **T** 944-234474, www.bidaideak.org, is an organization for the disabled, based in Bilbao.

Doctors
Clínica San Sebastián, C Rafael Ibarra 25, Bilbao, **T** 944-755000. **Centro de Salud Central**, C Santiago, 7-1º, Vitoria, **T** 945-258233. **Centro de Salud Gros**, C José Arana 7, San Sebastián, **T** 943-276199.

Electricity
Spain, as most of Europe, runs on 220V AC, with a two-pin plug.

Emergency numbers
The **emergency** number is **T** 112. Dial **T** 091 for the local **police** force and **T** 085 for an **ambulance**.

Hospitals
Hospital de Basurto, Av Montevideo 18, Bilbao, **T** 944-006000.
Hospital Nuestra Señora de Arantzazu, Av Doctor Begiristain
115, San Sebastián, **T** 943-007000. **Hospital Txagorritxu**, C José
Atxotegui s/n, Vitoria, **T** 945-007000.

Internet
Laser Internet, C Sendeja 5, Bilbao, **T** 944-453509, Mon-Fri
1030-0230, Sat and Sun 1100-0230, €0.05 per min, also
photocopying and fax services. **Web Press**, C Barrancua 11,
Bilbao, daily 1000-2230. **Donosti-Net**, C Embeltrán 2 and C San
Jerónimo 8, San Sebastián, **T** 943-429497, daily 0900-2300, €3 per
hr, also offers a left-luggage service. **Link Internet**, C San Antonio
31, Vitoria, **T** 945-130484, Mon-Fri 1000-1400 and 1730-2130, Sat
1030-1400, €2.10 per hr.

Language schools
Instituto Hemingway, C Bailén 5, Bilbao, **T** 944-167901,
www.institutohemingway.com.
Lacunza Escuela Internacional, Camino de Mundaiz 8, San
Sebastián, **T** 943-326680, www.lacunza.com.

Laundry
Tintoreria Lavaclin, Campo de Volantín 15, Bilbao, bag wash for
€10. **Wash'n Dry**, C Iparragirre 6, San Sebastián, **T** 943-293150.

Left luggage
There are *consignas* at all the major train stations in the region.

Libraries
Biblioteca Municipal, C Bidebarrieta 4, Bilbao, **T** 944-156930,
Mon-Fri 0930-2100, Sat 0930-1400.

Lost property

There's a dedicated lost property line, **T** 944-204981, but it's worth contacting the local police station, too.

Newspapers

The press is generally of a high journalistic standard. The national dailies *El País*, *El Mundo*, and the rightist *ABC* lose out in the Basque lands to *El Correo*, a quality Bilbao based syndicated chain. *El Diario Vasco* is another Basque daily, while *Egin* and *Deia* are papers half-published in Euskara with a blatantly nationalist bias.

Pharmacies (late-night)

Pharmacies in Euskadi operate on a rotating late-opening shift There's a list of the current rota in the window of every pharmacy.

Police

Emergencies, **T** 112. **Local police**, **T** 091. **Policía Municipal Bilbao**, C Luis Briñas 14, **T** 944-205000. **Policía Municipal San Sebastián**, C Larramendi 10, **T** 943-450000. **Policía Municipal Vitoria**, C Aguirrelanda s/n, **T** 945-161111.

Post offices

Main post offices (Alameda Urquijo 19, Bilbao; Paseo de Francia s/n, San Sebastián; C de Postas 9, Vitoria) are open Mon-Fri 0830-2030; some are also open Sat 0930-1400. Stamps can be bought at post offices or tobacconists (*estancos*).

Public holidays

See p197 for local holidays. Euskadi-wide holidays are:
1 Jan, New Year; **19 Mar**, San José; **Maundy Thursday**; **Good Friday**; **Easter Monday**; **1 May**, Labour Day; **25 Jul**, Santiago; **31 Jul**, San Ignacio (not Alava); **5 Aug**, Virgen Blanca (Alava only); **15 Aug**, Asunción; **12 Oct**, National Day; **1 Nov**, All Saints' Day; **6 Dec**, Constitution Day; **25 Dec**, Christmas Day.

Telephone
The international dialling code for Spain is +34. To make an international call from Spain, dial 00 followed by the relevant country code. Calls within Spain begin with a three digit area code, which must be dialled in all cases, even for local calls. Mobile numbers begin with 6. Public phones accept coins and cards, and all can be used for international direct dialling. *Locutorios* (call centres) are few and far between.

Time
Spain is one hour ahead of GMT, and puts its clocks forward and back at the same time as the UK and the rest of Europe.

Toilets
Public toilets are reasonably common, some are coin operated. In addition, staff will rarely object to you using the facilities in a bar, as long as you ask first. Toilets may be indicated by any of the following: '*Aseos*', '*Baños*', '*Komunak*', '*Servicios*' or '*HHSS*'.

Travel agents
Eroski Bidaiak, C Licenciado Poza 10, Bilbao, **T** 944-439012; C Igentea 2, San Sebastián, **T** 943-429740. **Viajes Ecuador**, Gran Vía 81, Bilbao, **T** 902-207070; Av Gasteiz 34, Vitoria, **T** 945-132144.

A sprint through history

Prehistory	Evidence of human presence in the Basque region goes back more than 50,000 years. Cave paintings suggest a continuous habitation since 10,000 BC.
71 BC	The Roman general Pompey campaigns in the area against the rogue general Quintus Sertorius, who had set himself up as a local warlord. He founds Pamplona, naming it after himself.
AD 581	The Visigoths fight several battles against the Basques, trying to pacify the peninsula.
778	Charlemagne campaigns in Navarra and, returning to France, his rearguard is ambushed by Basques in the Pyrenees. The resulting battle gave rise to the *Chanson de Roland*.
1004	Sancho the Great ascends the throne of Navarra, founds Vitoria and unites a large region.
1200	Alava and much of Guipúzcoa are taken by the crown of Castile, where they remain.
1300	Bilbao is granted its town charter by Don Diego López de Haro. It begins to flourish as a port for exporting goods produced in the interior.
1522	Juan Sebastián Elkano, from Getaria, becomes the first to circumnavigate the globe after the death of his captain Magellan in the Philippines.
1534	The Basque dandy Iñigo de Loyola, recovering from horrible injuries, has a series of religious revelations and founds the Company of Jesus, or Jesuits.
1728	The Real Compañia Guipúzcoana de Caracas is founded to monopolize the import of chocolate.

1813	The Peninsular War. The French garrison in San Sebastián is finally defeated. British and Portuguese troops set fire to the town, most of which is destroyed. The French are later routed just outside Vitoria, signalling an end to their Spanish campaign.
1833-39	First Carlist War. The Basques are heavily involved in this civil war, which arises out of a dispute over the succession. The conservative Carlists, who have supporters in the Basque agricultural towns, besiege liberal Bilbao, but are ultimately unsuccessful.
1841	As punishment for their support of the Carlists, the liberal government more or less ends Basque autonomy after the war.
1845	The beginning of Bilbao's big boom; Vizcaya becomes the premier source of haematite, the most effective ore for steel making.
1872-1876	Second Carlist War. At the end of the war the Basque *fueros* (privileges) are completely abolished.
1890	Sabino Arana publishes a work that becomes the foundation of Basque nationalism. He also devises the *ikurriña* (Basque flag) and the name Euskadi.
1903	Great Strike of Bilbao. The good times end.
1913 1929	Iron output halves.
1936	Spanish Civil War. The first Basque government is installed under Aguirre on 7 October after he pledges to support the Republicans.

1937	The brutal bombings of civilians at Durango and Gernika are carried out by Nationalist forces in late April. In June, Bilbao is taken by the Nationalists and the Basques surrender, although many fight on in other regions, and against Hitler in the Second World War.
1952	ETA is founded by young Basques, disenchanted by European and American recognition of Franco.
1973	Admiral Carrero Blanco, prime minister and Franco's right-hand man, is killed by an ETA car bomb; his assassination that meets with massive public support.
1975	Franco dies after nearly four decades of repression of the Basque region, in retribution for their support of the Republicans during the Civil War.
1980	Semi-autonomy is granted to the Basque region, and, separately, to Navarra. The regions have power to raise their own taxes, have their own police force, and control public works and education. Many Basques are satisfied with this concession, but ETA continues its programme of violence.
1997	The Guggenheim Museum opens in Bilbao.
2002-2004	Batasuna, the political party widely seen as a backer of ETA activities, is banned following a custom-designed bill passed by the Spanish parliament. A wave of arrests seems to subdue ETA. The PSOE government, elected in 2004, suggest it is open to the possibility of dialogue.

Art and architecture

Roman-esque (11th-12th century)
A fusion of styles combining features of Roman, Visigothic and local architecture, mainly spread through the church. Vaulted stone roofs made for less flammable buildings, which usually have small round-arched door and window openings, often featuring carved decoration. Even the larger structures have a warm and homely aspect, contrasting with the more austere and remote Gothic style that followed. There are numerous small romanesque chapels in the Basque countryside: one of the grander examples is the basilica of San Prudencio in Vitoria (Armentia).

Gothic (13th to mid-16th century)
Inspired by France and boosted by the unification of the peninsula, its primary features are pointed arches and rib-vaulting, which had been used sparingly in romanesque buildings. Advances in engineering allowed lighter, higher structures, supported by exterior flying buttresses. Becoming ever finer and more elaborate it incorporated stained glass and intricate carved sculptures. Gothic art, characterized by ornate coloured *retablos* (altarpieces), developed primarily through the religious medium. While today Gothic architecture is widely considered supreme in elegance and execution, the term was originally pejorative, meaning 'barbarous'.

Renaissance (16th century)
The Spanish renaissance style was influenced by Italian artists and became more grandiose, intricate and, some would say, pompous, over time. Vitoria and Oñati have some excellent examples.

Baroque (17th-18th century)	This period was a time of great architectural and artistic genius in Spain and the Basque country. The churrigueresque architectural style went even further down the ornamental path. Baroque *retablos* were frequently gilded and contrast sharply with the Gothic churches in which they're often found.
Neoclassical (mid 18th-19th century)	A reaction against the excesses of baroque, this sober style called on classical models to produce severe but harmonious civil and religious architecture, such as the Plaza Nueva in Bilbao. Much of the 'new towns' of the Basque cities are in this style.
Art nouveau and art deco (late 19th-mid 20th century)	Art nouveau aimed to bring art back to life and back to the everyday. Using naturalistic motifs to create whimsical façades and *objets*, the best art nouveau combines elegance with fancy. Art deco developed between the World Wars and was based on geometric forms, using new materials and colour combinations to create a popular style. San Sebastián is a temple to art nouveau and, like Bilbao, also has many good examples of art deco.
Modern	Suppressed or in exile during the Franco era, Basque art and architecture has flourished since the dictator's demise. The late Basque sculptors Chillida and Oteiza are globally admired, while the Guggenheim Museum, Artium and Kursaal have set the architectural tone for the 21st century.

ETA and Basque nationalism

Viewed in the context of a changing Europe, Basques have a strong case for independence, being culturally and ethnically distinct from Spaniards. The issue is muddied by the large number of Spaniards living in the Basque region but the real sticking point is that Spain has no intention of giving up such a profitable part of the nation. Economics don't permit it, old-fashioned Spanish honour doesn't permit it and, cleverly, the constitution doesn't permit it. Basque independence isn't going to happen and most Basques know it. From this frustration is born extremism among a small minority. While the overwhelming majority of Basque nationalists are firmly committed to a peaceful and democratic path, ETA is pessimistic about the possibility of achieving its aims through political means and seeks by planned violent action to force the issue.

The nationalist movement was founded in the late 19th century by Sabino Arana, a perceptive but unpleasant bigot who was a master of propaganda. He devised the *ikurriña* (the Basque flag), coined terms such as Euskadi and published manifestos for independence, peppered with dubious historical interpretations. The tragically short-lived breakthrough came with the Civil War, when the sundered Republic granted the Basques extensive self-government. José Antonio Aguirre was installed as *lehendakari* (leader) at Gernika on 7 October, 1936, and pledged Basque support for the struggle against Fascism. The government was forced into exile a few months later when Franco's Nationalists took Bilbao but Basques fought on in Spain and later in France against the Nazis.

At the end of the Second World War, Franco was ostracized by the USA and Europe, and the Basque government in exile was recognized as legitimate by the Western powers. However, as the Cold War grew ever chillier, the USA began to see the value of the anti-communist Franco and granted him a massive aid package. France and Britain followed suit, recognizing the Fascist government at the expense of the Basques and the Republican government-in-exile.

ETA was founded as ATA shortly after this sordid political turnabout. Its original goal was simply to promote Basque culture in repressive Spain but it soon took on a violent edge. In 1959 it took the name ETA (after realizing that *ata* meant duck in a Euskaran dialect), which stands for 'Euskadi Ta Askatasuna' ('the Basque Country and Freedom'). The group carried out its first assassination in 1968 and, since then, has been responsible for over 800 deaths, mostly of right-wing politicians, Basque 'collaborators' and police. It uses extortion and donations to fund its activities. ETA's current demands are autonomy for the Basque region, union with Navarra and the transfer of all Basque prisoners to prisons within the region. While this is a legitimate cause, there's nothing noble about ETA's normal *modus operandi*. In many cases it seems that the central leadership has little control over its trigger-happy thugs, and many of ETA's victims have been people with little or no political power.

For many years, the government and police were in a vicious and self-defeating cycle of violence with ETA: whenever the terrorist group struck, their support dropped dramatically, only to rise again a few days later, following the mystery retaliatory killing of Basques. The Socialist government of the early 1990s was found to have been funding a 'death squad' aimed at scaring Basques out of supporting the nationalist cause, and Basque prisoners have been routinely tortured in Guardia Civil jails. In 2002, the Madrid parliament passed legislation specifically and successfully designed to ban Batasuna, the political party often (and probably accurately) linked with ETA. During the same period, the police embarked on a campaign against ETA, with many high-profile arrests and discovery of arms caches. The attitude of the general public has also turned sharply since ETA's glory days in the 1970s. The World Trade Center and Madrid train bombings mean that any terrorist action is now seen as appalling.

ETA has kept fairly quiet in the 21st century and the present PSOE government of José Luís Rodríguez Zapatero is more disposed to negotiate so, for the first time in many years, there is some hope for an end to the conflict.

Euskara

Euskara is an ancient and complex language with no known relatives. Like Finnish, it is agglutinative, meaning roughly that distinct bits are joined on to words for each element of meaning. In Basque the tense, person, number, mood, mode and aspect are all represented by different additions, which results in numerous variations of a single word. People struggle with seven cases in Latin, but Basque has a massive 20. Euskara is pronounced as it is written, with these main exceptions: *x* is "sh", s is almost lisped as is the slightly harder *z* sound, *h* is usually silent. The *eu* diphthong is pronounced as a quick "ay-oo".

Basic phrases

Hello	*¡kaixo!*
Hello/goodbye	*Agur*
Yes	*Bai*
No	*Ez*
Welcome	*Ongi-etorri*
Please	*Mesedez*
Thank you	*Eskerrik asko*
Excuse me	*Parkatu*
Toilets	*Komunak*
Beach	*Hondartza*
Street	*Kale*
House	*Etxe* (many words derive from this root)
Guesthouse (*pensión*)	*Ostatua*
Farmhouse	*Baserri*
Ciderhouse	*Sagardotegi*
Restaurant	*Jatetxea*
Wine	*Ardo*
Water	*Ura*
Beer	*Garagardo*

Castellano

Greetings, courtesies
The following phrases use the informal '*tú*' form of the verb.
Good morning   *buenos días*
How are you?   *¿cómo estás?*
Pleased to meet you   *mucho gusto/encantado/encantada*
What is your name?   *¿Cómo te llamas?*
I am called   *me llamo…*
Excuse me/I beg your pardon/sorry   *permiso/disculpe*
I do not understand   *no entiendo*
please speak slowly   *hablas despacio por favor*
I don't speak Spanish   *no hablo castellano*
Do you speak English?   *¿Hablas inglés?*

Money
bill   *la cuenta*
cheap   *barato*
credit card   *la tarjeta de crédito*
exchange house   *la casa de cambio*
exchange rate   *la tasa de cambio*
expensive   *caro*
How much does it cost?   *¿Cuánto cuesta?*

Getting around
Where is?   *¿Dónde está?*
corner   *la esquina*
How do I get to_?   *¿Cómo llegar a_?*
on the left/right   *a la izquierda/derecha*
straight on   *derecho*
walk   *caminar*
When does the bus leave/arrive?   *¿A qué hora sale/llega el autobus?*
Where can I buy tickets?   *¿Dónde se puede comprar billetes?*

Accommodation

clean/dirty towels *las toallas limpias/sucias*
Have you got a room for two people? *¿tiene* (formal)/*tienes* (informal) *habitación para dos personas?*
Is service included? *¿Está incluido el servicio?*
pillows *las almohadas*
sheets *las sábanas*
shower *la ducha*
single/twin/double *individual/doble/doble de matrimonio*
to make up/clean *limpiar*
toilet paper *el papel higiénico*
with private bathroom *con baño*
with two beds *con dos camas*

Time

At half past two/ two thirty *a las dos y media*
At a quarter to three *a las tres menos cuarto*
It's seven o'clock *son las siete*
It's twenty past six/six twenty *son las seis y veinte*
It's five to nine *son las nueve menos cinco*
In ten minutes *en diez minutos*
five hours *cinco horas*
Does it take long? *¿Tarda mucho?*
We will be back at *Regresamos a las…*
What time is it? *¿Qué hora es?*
Monday *lunes*
Tuesday *martes*
Wednesday *miércoles*
Thursday *jueves*
Friday *viernes*
Saturday *sábado*
Sunday *domingo*

Barolo a pil pil — yellow same

Food glossary

This is by no means a definitive list. See also p159.

Aceitunas   Olives

Ajo   Garlic

Alcachofa   Artichoke

Alioli   A sauce of raw garlic blended with oil and egg yolk

Almejas   Name applied to various species of small clams

Alubias   Beans

Anchoa   Preserved anchovy. *Boquerones* are fresh anchovies

Arroz   Rice

Asado   Roast

Bacalao   Salt cod; *al ajo arriero* is mashed with garlic, parsley, paprika

Berenjena   Aubergine/eggplant

Bonito   Atlantic bonito, a small tasty tuna fish

Cabrales   A delicious Asturian cheese similar to Roquefort

Cacahuetes   Peanuts

Café   Coffee. *Solo* is black, served espresso-style; *cortado* adds a dash of milk, *con leche* more; *Americano* is a long black

Cazuela   A stew, often of fish or seafood

Cerdo   Pork

Cerveza   Beer. *Una caña* is a draught beer; *un zurito* is a short beer

Chuleta/Chuletilla   Chop

Cochinillo/Lechón/Tostón   Suckling pig

Cocido   A heavy stew, usually of meat and beans

Cordero   Lamb

Costillas   Ribs

Cuajada   Junket (a thin natural yoghurt) eaten with honey

Dorada   gilthead bream

Embutido   Any salami-type sausage

Filete   Steak. *Poco hecho* is rare, *al punto* is medium rare, *regular* is medium, *muy hecho* is well-done. *Solomillo* is sirloin steak

Foie   Fattened liver

Gambas   Prawns

Garbanza   Chickpea

Guisado   Stewed, or a stew
Higado   Liver
Lechazo   Milk-fed lamb
Lenguado   Sole
Lubina   Sea bass
Marisco   Shellfish
Mejillones   Mussels
Menestra   A vegetable stew, often seeded with ham and pork
Merluza   Hake is to Spain as rice is to southeast Asia
Morcilla   Blood sausage
Mosto   Grape juice, a common option in bars
Pan   Bread
Pato   Duck
Patxarán   Sloe berry, but usually the liqueur made from it
Pollo   Chicken
Postre   Dessert
Pulga   Tiny submarine-shaped rolls that feature as bar top snacks
Pulpo   Octopus
Queso   Cheese
Rabo de buey   Oxtail
Rape   Monkfish
Relleno/a   Stuffed
Revuelto   Scrambled eggs, usually with mushrooms or seafood
Rodaballo   Turbot. Pricey and toothsome
Romana (à la)   Fried in batter
Sal   Salt
Setas   Wild mushrooms, often superb
Sidra   Cider
Sopa   Soup
Ternera   Veal or young beef
Trucha   Trout
Ttoro   A traditional Basque fish stew or soup
Txaka   A mixture of mayonnaise and chopped seafood
Vizcaína (à la)   Sauce based on onions and dried peppers

241

Books

Atxaga, **B**, *Obabakoak* (1994), Vintage Books. A dreamlike, anecdotal novel by a well-respected contemporary Basque author.

Baroja, **P**, *The Tree of Knowledge* (1911). Mostly set in Madrid and Valencia, this is the best introduction to this powerful Basque novelist.

Barrenechea, **T**, *The Basque Table* (1998), Harvard Common Press. A cookbook with tons of traditional Basque recipes.

Carr, **R** (ed), *Spain: A History* (2000), Oxford University Press. An interesting compilation of recent writing on Spanish history, with plenty of perspective on Basque issues.

Kurlansky, **M**, *The Basque History of the World* (1999), Vintage Press. A likeable introduction to what makes the Basques tick: their food, history and characteristics. Informal, fireside style.

Rankin, N, *Telegram from Guernica* (2003). A biography of George Steer (see below) with great descriptions of wartime Bilbao.

Steer, **G**, *The Tree of Guernica* (1938), Hodder and Stoughton. Written by a pro-Republican reporter who was an eyewitness to the atrocity of the Gernika bombing.

Unamuno, **M**, *Tragic Sense of Life* (1913), Dover Publications (1990). The great Basque and Salamantine philosopher tries to come to terms with faith and death. Earlier work, written in Bilbao in the late 19th century, reflects the fervent cultural atmosphere of the time.

Zulaika, **J**, *Basque Violence: Metaphor and Sacrament* (2000), University of Nevada Press. Academic but intriguing exploration of the roots of Basque nationalism and the progression to violence.

Index

Credits

Footprint credits
Text editor: Sophie Blacksell
Map editor: Sarah Sorensen

Publisher: Patrick Dawson
Series created by: Rachel Fielding
In-house cartography: Claire Benison,
Robert Lunn
Proof-reading: Sarah Sorensen

Design: Mytton Williams
Maps: adapted by Footprint from original
cartography by Netmaps SA, Barcelona,
Spain. Metro map reproduced with
permission of Metro Bilbao, 2006

Photography credits
Front cover: Superstock (*Maman*
outside the Guggenheim)
Black and white images: Andy Symington
(p1 Guggenheim and *Maman*, p31
Guggenheim, p63 bridge at Ondarroa),
Superstock (p5 *pelota* balls).
Generic images: John Matchett
Back cover: Superstock (Playa de la
Concha, San Sebastián)

Print
Manufactured in Italy by LegoPrint
Pulp from sustainable forests.

Publishing information
Footprint Bilbao & the Basque country
2nd edition
Text and maps © Footprint Handbooks
Ltd March 2006

ISBN 1 904777 79 1
CIP DATA: a catalogue record for this
book is available from the British Library

Published by Footprint Handbooks
6 Riverside Court
Lower Bristol Road
Bath, DA2 3DZ, UK
T +44 (0)1225 469141
F +44 (0)1225 469461
discover@footprintbooks.com
www.footprintbooks.com

Distributed in the USA by
Publishers Group West

® Footprint Handbooks and the Footprint
mark are a registered trademark of
Footprint Handbooks Ltd

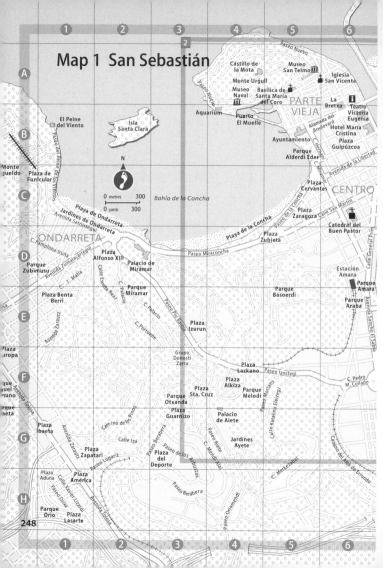

Map 1 San Sebastián

Maps

Bilbao Metro, inside
front cover.
1 San Sebastián, p248.
2 San Sebastián centre, p250.
3 Bilbao, p252.
4 Bilbao – El Ensanche,
the riverbank
& Deusto, p254.
5 Bilbao – Casco Viejo, p256.
6 Basque country, inside
back cover.

Map symbols

- 🚌 Bus station
- ➡️ Train station
- Ⓜ Metro
- 🚋 Tram
- Ⓔ Euskotren
- ⧓ Funicular
- ⛪ Cathedral, church
- ➕ Hospital
- Ⓜ Market
- 🏛 Museum
- ✉ Post office
- ℹ Tourist information
- ◣ Related map
- ◣ Detail map

Map 2 San Sebastián centre

250

Monte Urgull

Castillo de la Mota

Museo Naval

Aquarium

Jacques Cousteau

Puerto

El Muelle

Plaza Castillo

Subida al Castillo

Paseo Nuevo

Paseo del Muelle

Paseo Molino

Bahía de la Concha

Basílica de Santa María del Coro

Museo de San Telmo

Iglesia San Vicente

PARTE VIEJA

La Bretxa

Ayuntamiento

Alameda del Boulevard

Teatro Victoria Eugenia

Paseo Ramón María Lili

Pte. Sta. Catalina

Pte. Zurriola

Kursaal

Avenida Zurriola

Playa de Zurriola

GROS

Plaza Padre Claret

Plaza Lapurdi

Avenida

Chofre

Plaza Euskal Herria

Plaza Navarroa

Plaza Cataluña

Plaza Biteri

Plaza Pinares

C. San Cristóbal

Estación del Norte

Avenida de Francia

Plaza Teresa de Calcuta

Plaza Hirutxulo

Plaza Blas Otero

Arbol de Guernica

CENTRO

Plaza Bilbao

Catedral del Buen Pastor

Hotel María Cristina

Jardines de Oquendo

Plaza de Guipúzcoa

Plaza España

Avenida de la Libertad

Calle San Martín

C. Miramar

C. Hernani

Paseo de la Concha

Playa de la Concha

Bahía de la Concha

Parque Alderdi Eder

Plaza Zubieta

Plaza José Arana

Plaza Vinuesa

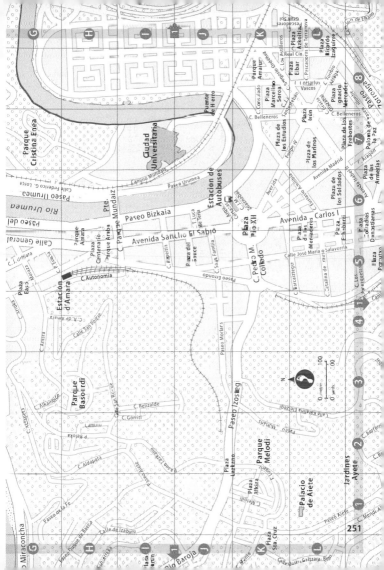

251

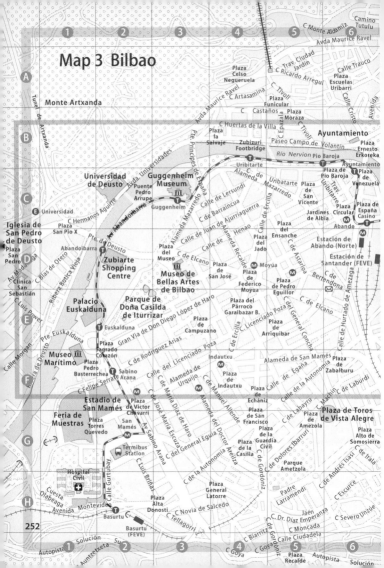

Map 3 Bilbao

A

Monte Artxanda

B

Tunel de Artxanda

Universidad de Deusto

C

E Universidad

Iglesia de San Pedro de Deusto

Plaza San Pedro

D

Clínica San Sebastián

Av Lehendakari Aguirre

C Blas de Otero

C Luis Power

E

Calle Morgan

Pta de Deusto

Palacio Euskalduna

Pte. Euskalduna

Plaza Pedro Basterrechea

Euskalduna

T Sabino Arana

Ribera Botica Vieja

Abandoibarra

Plaza San Pío X

C Hermanos Aguirre

Avda. Universidades

Puente Pedro Arrupe

Guggenheim Museum

Guggenheim

T Zubiarte Shopping Centre

Museo de Bellas Artes de Bilbao

Parque de Doña Casilda de Iturrizar

Plaza Sagrado Corazón

Camino Tutulu

C Monte Aldámiz

Avda Maurice Ravel

Trav. Ciudad Jardín

C Ricardo Arregui

Calle Trauco

Plaza Escuelas Uribarri

Plaza Celso Neguerela

Avda Maurice Ravel

C Artasamina

C Tívoli

Plaza Tívoli

C Castaños

Plaza Funicular

Plaza Moraza

C Tívoli

Calle Cristo

Avenida

C Huertas de la Villa

Plaza fa Salvaje

Zubizuri Footbridge

Pte. Príncipes de España

Paseo Campo de Volantín

Ayuntamiento

Plaza Ernesto Erkoreka

Río Nervión Pío Baroja

T Baroja

T Ayuntamiento

Uribitarte

C. de Alameda

Uribatarte Mazarredo

Plaza de San Vicente

Plaza de Pío Baroja

Plaza de Venezuela

Alda. Mazarredo

C. de Lersundi

C. de Barraincúa

Calle de Juan de Ajurriaguerra

C. de Alameda Recalde

Henao

Jardines de Albia

Plaza Circular

T

Abando

Plaza de España Casino

M

Estación de Abando (Norte)

Estación de Santander (FEVE)

Plaza del Museo

C. de Elcano

Plaza de San José

Plaza del Ensanche

Plaza del Jado

M Moyúa

C. de Astarloa

C. de Bertendona

C. de Hurtado de Amézaga

Plaza de Federico Moyúa

Plaza de Pedro Eguillor

C. de Elcano

Museo Marítimo

Plaza de Victor Chávarri

Estadio de San Mamés

Feria de Muestras

Plaza Torres Quevedo

San Mamés

M

T

C Felipe Serrate

Gran Vía de Don Diego López de Haro

Plaza de Campuzano

Plaza del Párroco Garaibazar B.

Plaza de Arriquibar

Plaza de Ercilla

C de General Concha

C del Licenciado Poza

Indautxu M

C de Rodríguez Arias

C de Licenciado Poza

C. de Manuel Allende

Alameda de Urquijo

M

Plaza de Indautxu

Alameda de San Mamés

C. de Égaña

Calle de la Autonomía

Plaza de Zabalburu

C. de María Díaz de Haro

C. de José María Escuza

Av. Sabino Arana

C del General Eguía

Plaza de San Francisco

Plaza de Echániz

Plaza de Amézola

C de Labayru

M de Laburdi

Plaza de Toros de Vista Alegre

Plaza Alto de Somosierra

Ría de Bilbao

Plaza San Mamés

Termibus Station

Hospital Civil

C Luis Gurtubay

Plaza Alta Donosti

Cuesta Olabeaga

Avenida Montevideo

Basurtu

Basurtu (FEVE)

C del General Eguía

Plaza de la Casilla

Plaza de la Guardia Civil

C de Gordoníz

C de Dolores Ibarruri

Parque Ametzola

Plaza General Latorre

C Novia de Salcedo

C Tellagorri

C de Biarritz

Jaén

Padre Larramendi

C. Dr. Díaz Emperanza

C de Goya

Calle Ciudadela

C Escurce

C de Andrés Isasi C de Irala

C Severo Unzue

C Moncada

Plaza Recalde

Plaza Alegre

Map 4 Bilbao
El Ensanche, the riverbank & Deusto

Universidad de Deusto

Guggenheim Museum

Puente Pedro Arrupe

Guggenheim

Universidad

Subida Buena Vista

Plaza San Pío X

Calle Hermanos Aguirre

Pte. de Deusto

Calle de Elcano

DEUSTO

Iglesia de San Pedro de Deusto

Plaza San Pedro

Abandoibarra

Zubiarte Shopping Centre

Plaza del Museo

Museo de Bellas Artes de Bilbao

Avenida Lehendakari

Avenida Madariaga

Calle Rafaela Ybarra

Calle Heliodoro Otero

Ribera Botica Vieja

Plaza de Teófilo Guiard

Clínica San Sebastián

Parque de Doña Casilda de Iturrízar

Deustu

Palacio Euskalduna

Gran Vía de Don Diego López de Haro

Plaza de Campuzano

Euskalduna

Paseo de J. Anselmo Clavé

Calle Jon de Arrospide

Pte. Euskalduna

Plaza Sagrado Corazón

Museo Marítimo Ría de Bilbao

Sabino Arana

Plaza Pedro Basterrechea

Feria de Muestras

Estadio de San Mamés

Plaza de Víctor Chávarri

254

0 metres 100
0 yards 100

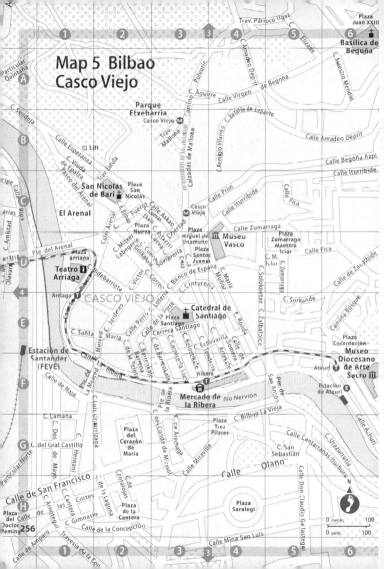

Map 5 Bilbao
Casco Viejo

Plaza
Juan XXIII

Basílica de
Begoña

Trav. Párroco Ugaz

C. Elzate

C. Maestro Mendiri

C. Amadeo Deprit

C. Aguirre

Calle Virgen de Begoña

Camino Polvorín

C. Sendeja

Parque
Etxebarria

Casco Viejo

Trav.
Mallona

Calzadas de Mallona

C. Remigio Vilariño 2

Calle Batalla de Lepanto

Calle Amadeo Deprit

Calle Begoña Azpi

Calle Iturribide

Calle Esperanza

C. Viuda
de Spalza

Paseo del Arenal

Trav. Etuña

Lift

San Nicolás
de Bari

Plaza
San
Nicolás

Calle Prim

Calle Iturribide

Calle Fica

Calle Fica

El Arenal

Calle Arenal

C. Bilbao

Fueros

Calle Cuevas

Elcani

Calle Askao

Calle Ronda

Libertad

Plaza
Nueva

Calle Zumarraga

Casco
Viejo

Plaza
Miguel de
Unamuno

Museo
Vasco

Plaza
Zumarraga
Maestro
Iciar

Calle Fica

C. Mitxer

Labegoie

C. Cruz

Sombrerría

Plaza
Santos
Juanes

C. Iturriza

C. María
Muñoz

Calle Zumarraga

C. Iclur

Ptre. del Arenal

Plaza
Arriaga

Teatro
Arriaga

Bidebarrieta

C. Víctor

C. Correo

Banco de España

Cinturería

Solokoetxe

C. Zabalbide

Calle Zurkunde

Camino Bosque

Arriaga

CASCO VIEJO

C. Santa

C. Merced

C. María

C. Jardines

Calle Perro

C. Lotería

C. de la Torre

Catedral de
Santiago

Plaza
Santiago

Correra Santiago

C. Rondá

Calle
Somera

C. Echevarria

Calle
Tendería

Plaza
Encarnación

Museo
Diocesano
de Arte
Sacro

Estación de
Santander
(FEVE)

Calle de La Ribera

C. de la Merced

Calle de Naja

C. Luis Urrutizaga

C. Barrenkale

C. Barrenkalebarrena

C. Carnicería Vja.

Ribera

Arteakle

Atxuri

Ptre. de San Antón

Estación
de Atxuri

Calle Achuri

Mercado de
la Ribera

Río Nervión

C. Lamana

C. Dos de Mayo

C. Hernani

C. de la Laguna

C. e Arechaga

Plaza
del
Corazón
de
María

C. e de
Cantolado

Plaza Tres
Pilares

Calle Bilbao La Vieja

Calle Cantarranas Iturburu

C. Urazurrutia

C. del Gral. Castillo

Plaza
del
Conde
de Mirasol

Calle Miravilla

C. San
Sebastián

Calle Don Claudio Gallastegui

Calle de San Francisco

Plaza
del
Calle
Doctor
Fleming

256

C. Amparo

C. Cantera

C. Cortes

C. Amézteguí

C. Gimnasio

Plaza
de la
Cantera

Calle de la Concepción

Calle

Plaza
Saralegi

Olano

Travesía de la Con

Calle de Amparo

Calle Mina San Luis

N

0 metres   100
0 yards   100

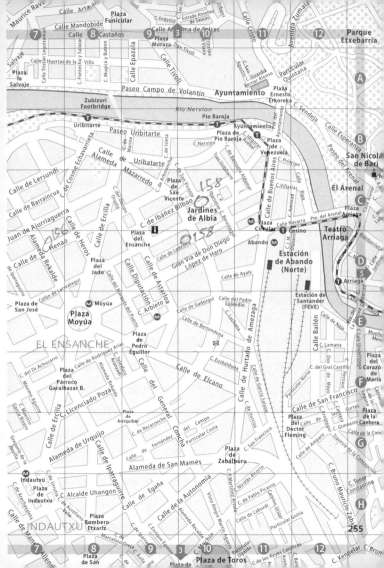